SULPHIDES

SULP

THE ART OF CA

PAU

GALAHAD BOOKS · NEW YOR

HIDES
O INCRUSTATION

JOKELSON

Door plaques by Apsley Pellatt. *Author's Collection*

© 1968 by Paul Jokelson
All rights reserved under International and Pan-American Conventions.
Published in New York by Thomas Nelson & Sons.
Library of Congress Catalog Card Number: 73-90834
ISBN 0-88365-134-3
Published by arrangement with Thomas Nelson & Sons
Printed in the United States of America
Design by Harold Leach

To my wife
for her constant encouragement
and wonderful help
which made this
book possible

ACKNOWLEDGMENTS

One of the most difficult tasks in writing this book is no doubt to express as I wish I could my heartfelt thanks and gratitude to all the persons—some friends of long standing, some known only through correspondence—who have given me their advice, their help and encouragement. I am deeply grateful to Mr. Raoul de Broglie, Curator, Musée Condé, Chantilly, France; Mademoiselle Marcelle Brunet, Librarian, Manufacture Nationale de Sèvres, France; Mrs. E. Campbell Cloak, Assistant Director, The John Bergstrom Museum and Art Center, Neenah, Wisconsin; R. J. Charleston, Esq., Keeper, Department of Ceramics, Victoria & Albert Museum, London, England; Mrs. George Ertell, Solana Beach, California; Mr. Gerard Hubert, Curator, Musée National de la Malmaison, Rueil-Malmaison, France; Mr. Gerard Ingold, Director, Cristalleries de Saint Louis, Saint-Louis, France; Mr. Frank Kireker, Jr., Ridgewood, N.J.; Mademoiselle Anne-Marie Labit, Curator, Musée d'Agen, France; Doctor Charles Lasserre, Bordeaux, France; Paul Loraine, Esq., London, England; Mr. Fred A. Nagel, Chicago, Illinois; R. Oddy, Esq., Assistant Keeper, The Royal Scottish Museum, Edinburgh, Scotland; Mr. J. Payen, Chef des Travaux, Conservatoire National des Arts & Métiers, Paris, France; Paul N. Perrot, Director, The Corning Museum of Glass, Corning, N.Y.; Mrs. Ada Polak, London, England; Mr. Albert Christian Revi, Managing Editor, Spinning Wheel, Hanover, Pa.; Mademoiselle Monique Ricour, Photographic Department, Musée des Arts Décoratifs, Paris, France; Mr. L. B. Sark, Greenwich, Conn.; Miss Vivian J. Scheidemantel, Associate Curator of Decorative Arts, The Art Institute of Chicago, Chicago, Illinois; Mrs. Carolyn Scoon, Assistant Director, The New York Historical Society, New York, N.Y.; Doctor Ake Setterwall, Surveyor of the Royal Collection, Royal Palace, Stockholm, Sweden; Mrs. F. J. Sisson, Charleston, West Virginia; Sotheby & Company, London, England; Mr. Edward S. Thompson, Maryville, Kentucky; Vicomte P. de Toulgoët, Paris, France; Mr. Xavier Védère, Curator, Musée des Arts Décoratifs, Bordeaux, France; Mr. Andre Vulliet, Vice-President, Baccarat, Inc., New York, N.Y.; Hugh Wakefield, Esq., Keeper of Circulation, Victoria & Albert Museum, London, England; Mr. Kenneth M. Wilson, Curator, The Corning Museum of Glass, Corning, N.Y.; and George A. Young, Esq., Superintendent of City Museums, Edinburgh, Scotland.

PREFACE

In her book, *Old Glass Paperweights* (Crown Publishers, New York, N.Y., 1940), Mrs. Evangeline H. Bergstrom wrote: "The study of ceramics is a field in itself, and one that invites much interesting historical research." We are in complete agreement with this statement and we have, for some time, been gathering material relating to "sulphides" in order to publish a book that would include everything of importance written on this subject since 1849, plus our recent discoveries and a large number of photographs of the finest pieces now in museums and private collections.

The first book mentioning this fascinating art was written by Apsley Pellatt (*Curiosities of Glass-Making*, London, 1849), who took a patent for "Crystallo-Ceramie" on June 17, 1819. A pamphlet was published in 1909 in France by J. P. Emperauger under the title: "Verres et cristaux incrustés" ("Incrusted glass and crystal") and a chapter is devoted to this art in Gustav E. Pazaurek's book *Glaser der Empire—Und Briedermeirzert* (Leipzig, 1923). It seems that all the other authors have largely borrowed from these three sources and we have followed the same path, combining text from the three works in such a way that it proved impractical to state after each sentence or paragraph the source of the information. We can therefore only gratefully acknowledge the great amount of research done by Apsley Pellatt, Commandant Emperauger, and Gustav E. Pazaurek and hope that, with a few additions of our own and some photographs, a complete story about "sulphides" will unfold for our readers.

Our interest in sulphides dates from the time we started collecting paperweights, in 1925, and found that, while it was relatively easy to acquire a fine paperweight, the sulphides were quite difficult to find. This is still true today. We have compiled Sotheby's catalogues from 1952 to 1967 and only 471 sulphides and color incrustations were offered for sale during these fifteen years: 238 paperweights, 96 plaques, 42 tumblers, 32 scent bottles, 14 doorknobs, 11 buttons, 12 letter weights, 12 patch boxes, 7 vases, 5 obelisks, and 2 salts. Since thousands of paperweights changed hands during that same period we can safely say that sulphides are comparatively rare.

Contrary to other objects of art, most of the "cameo incrustations" are closely related to historical events and famous persons, which gives them a special appeal to collectors. As Mrs. Lura Woodside Watkins wrote in an article on medallion paperweights: "There are few persons whose interest in glass is so completely abstract that they cannot be stirred to enthusiasm by pieces that have historical significance."

In trying to identify some of the sulphides that are reproduced in this book, we came to the conclusion that our knowledge of history and of historical characters could very well stand a refresher course. We felt that others also might like to refresh their memory or learn some facts previously ignored. The "Biography" is included here for those readers who are not only interested in the beauty of the sulphides but in the history of the people they represent.

At the end of the chapter about incrusted cameos, Pazaurek wrote: "Let us hope that the time is not far away when this kind of work, which has died out, will be resurrected in a new truly artistic spirit." This wish came true in 1952 when we prompted the Cristalleries de Baccarat and the Cristalleries de Saint Louis, France, to revive this lost art in the form of sulphide paperweights. We trust that artists worthy of Saint-Amans, Desprez, and Andrieu will combine their talents with the facilities of modern glass factories to perpetuate this great invention and produce lovely sulphides for future generations.

NOTE

There are practically no records of the sulphides made by the French factories and, except for some paperweights with mille-fiori canes, which help identify their origin, it is extremely difficult to give a positive identification of the objects with cameo incrustations produced by these factories. This is also true for works by Saint-Amans who did not sign his sulphides. We have tried to the best of our ability to identify the cameo incrustations illustrated in this book by comparing some of them with others positively identified and, when this proved impossible, we gave a tentative attribution followed by an interrogation mark. We hope that we have not made too many mistakes and that readers might correct the mistakes we may have made.

All photographs by Taylor & Dull, New York, N.Y., except as noted.

Roman numerals in the text refer to color plates.

CONTENTS

SULPHIDES

THE ART OF
CAMEO INCRUSTATION

The art of cameo under glass called "sulphide" comes from this observation that the "drops of rain or dew give a silvery aspect to the leaves which are villous and rough to the touch. From this it has been deduced that an unpolished object which does not melt at the temperature of crystal could, incrusted in its depth, simulate silver."

Apsley Pellatt described this art in *Curiosities of Glass-Making* (London, 1849): "The ancients were not altogether ignorant of the art of embodying ornaments in the interior of glass; but their productions were only partially enclosed. It was impossible to introduce into the interior of glass any device or figure, which could be with certainty accurately defined; because, the variegated glass in the interior being of the same nature as the enamel, is (especially if opaque) fusible at a less degree of heat than the coating of white transparent glass: consequently, any impression must have been effaced, when, in the process of manufacture, it became incased in the hot transparent glass. To render the art of incrustation subservient to any useful purpose, it was requisite, in the first instance, to discover a substance capable of uniting with glass, but requiring a stronger heat than its transparent enclosure to render it fusible.

"A Bohemian manufacturer first attempted, around 1750, to incrust in glass small figures of greyish clay. The experiments which he made, were in but few instances successful, in consequence of the clay not being adapted to combine completely with the glass. It was, however, from the Bohemian that the idea was caught by some French manufacturers, who, after having expended a considerable sum in the attempt, at length succeeded in incrusting several medallions of Buonaparte, which were sold at an enormous price. From the extreme difficulty of making these medallions, and from their almost invariably breaking while under the operation of cutting, very few were finished; and the manufacture was upon the point of being abandoned, when it was fortunately taken up by a French gentleman, Monsieur de St. Amans, who, with a perseverance not less honorable to himself than in its results advantageous to the arts, prosecuted a series of experiments, by which, in a few years, he very considerably improved the invention. The French have, however, not succeeded in introducing incrustation into articles of any size such as decanters, jugs or plates; but have contented themselves with ornamenting smelling-bottles, and small trinkets. Nor had the invention been applied to heraldry, or any other purpose, antecedently to the recent improvements upon the art in this country."

[Apsley Pellatt was mistaken or at least proven to be wrong later because large decanters, plaques, and incrusted medals were produced in France by Boudon de Saint-Amans, Baccarat, and Saint Louis: a number of them are illustrated in this book.—Author's note.]

ENGLISH SULPHIDES

"England has long been famed for bringing to perfection and directing to useful application, the crude inventions of other countries. A patent was, some years since, taken out by the author of this work for ornamental incrustations, called "Crystallo-Ceramie," which excited considerable notice at the time. By this process, ornaments of any description—coats of arms, ciphers, portraits, and landscapes of any variety of colour—are enclosed within the glass, so as to become chemically imperishable. The substance of which these ornaments are composed, is less fusible than glass; it is incapable of generating air, and at the same time is susceptible of contraction or expansion, as, in the course of manufacture, the glass becomes hot or cold. It may previously be formed into any device or figure, by either moulding or modelling; and may be painted with metallic colours, which are fixed by exposure to a melting heat. These ornaments are introduced within the body of the glass while the latter is hot, by which means the air is effectually excluded; the incrustation being thus actually incorporated in the glass. In this way, every description of ornamental glassware has been decorated with embossed, white, or coloured arms, or crests. Specimens of these incrustations have been exhibited not only in decanters and wine-glasses, but in lamps, girandoles, chimney ornaments, plates, and smelling-bottles. Busts and statues, on a small scale, caryatides to support lamps or clocks, and masks, after the antique, have also been introduced with admirable effect.

"The composition used in the patent incrustations is of a white silvery appearance, which has a superb effect when inclosed in richly-cut glass. Miniature landscapes have been enamelled upon it, without the colours losing any of their brilliancy; and thus, instead of being painted on the surface of the crystal, there are ornaments embodied in it.

"A second patent was subsequently secured by the author (September 9, 1831), by which medals, coats-of-arms, crests, etc., are accurately transferred from the dies on which they had been chased, to hollow glassware, especially where numerous repetitions of arms of elaborate workmanship are required. This invention diminishes the expense of engraving, in transferring the pattern by means of cakes of tripoli, from the die to services of glassware, and it has frequently been used with great advantage.

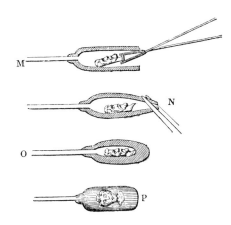

"Bas-relief casts of busts, and medals, were entirely isolated within a coating or mass of white flint glass. The figure intended for incrustation must be made of materials that will require a higher degree of heat from their fusion than the glass within which it is to be incrusted; these are china clay and supersilicate of potash, ground and mixed in such proportions as upon experiment harmonize with the density of the glass; and this, when moulded into a bas-relief, or bust, (in plaster of Paris moulds), should be slightly baked, and then suffered gradually to cool; or the cameos may be kept in readiness till required for incrustation, for which purpose they should be carefully reheated to redness in a small Stourbridge clay muffle. A cylindrical flint glass pocket is then prepared, one end adhering to the hollow iron rod, M, with an opening at the other extremity, into which the hot composition figure is introduced; the end, N, is then collapsed and welded together by pressure, at a red heat, so that the figure is in the centre of the hollow hot glass pocket or muffle. The workman next applies his mouth at the end of the tube, O, while rewarming the glass at the other extremity; but instead of blowing, he exhausts the air, thus perfecting the collapse, by atmospheric pressure, and causing the glass and composition figure to be of one homogeneous mass, as P.

"Small bas-reliefs and casts of coins or medals are incrusted in a more expeditious manner, and especially upon hollow glass vessels, by placing a hot prepared cameo, of the usual composition, upon the hot manufactured vessel; a small piece of liquid glass is dropped on it, and becomes welded; and if rubbed while hot, the upper coat of fused glass will be spread as thinly as possible upon and around the cameo, behind which are driven any air bubbles that may be entrapped; thus completely isolating the device between the two glasses. These incrustations require very careful annealing."

Figs. 1 & 2. These two drawings show how the 2-part or 3-part metal mould could be closed immediately before blowing. The use of pressed glass instead of cut glass simplified and made more economical the manufacture of incrustations.

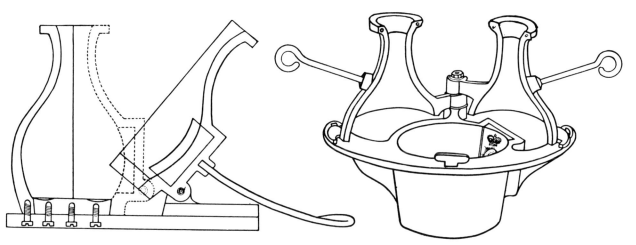

Figs. 3 & 4. (Left) Portrait of Princess Charlotte by Apsley Pellatt, after a painting by Challon. Princess Charlotte (1796-1817) was the daughter of George IV and wife of Leopold, afterwards King of Belgium. (Right) The reverse of this plaque is in color. *Author's Collection*

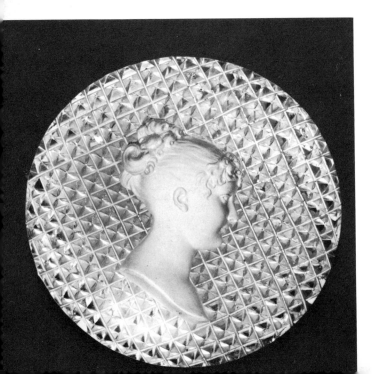

Fig. 5. Portrait of Queen Victoria by Apsley Pellatt (?). *Private Collection, Paris, Fance*

When one considers the minute size of some of the ornaments, for example earrings and rings, one realizes the extreme
delicacy of the process and can readily imagine how many must
have been broken in the making. (Fig. I and II.)

The refraction of the light through the glass has the strange
trick of making the cameo appear like silver. Many think the
clay must have been silvered or the cameo made of metal, but
this is not so. Unfortunately, Apsley Pellatt also made a great
deal of pressed glass and, like the French, favored the making
of imitations and substitutes. Meanwhile he constructed in
Holland Street, of the London suburb of Blackfriars Bridge,
a bottle-glass factory, and tried to make the incrustations in
a mechanical way. Both drawings (Figs. 1 and 2), which are
enclosed with the mentioned patent (No. 6091) of 1831, dem-
onstrate very well the two kinds of mould; how the 2-part or
3-part metal mould, when the incrustation medallion was

Fig. 6. Crystal flask with a sulphide
of George IV, King of England,
by Apsley Pellatt. *Collection of
Musée des Arts Décoratifs, Paris,
France*

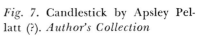

Fig. 7. Candlestick by Apsley Pellatt (?). *Author's Collection*

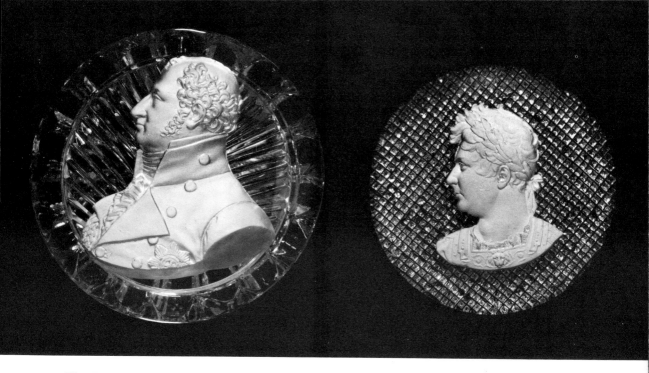

Fig. 8. (*Left*) Sweet box with sulphide of the Duke of York by Apsley Pellatt. (*Right*) George IV, King of England, by Pellatt and Green. *Author's Collection*

Fig. 9. (*Left*) George III, King of England, wearing the Order of the Garter. (*Right*) Unidentified man by Apsley Pellatt. *Author's Collection*

made ready, is closed immediately before blowing. It is quite evident that this simplified and economic method of manufacture favored the use of pressed glass instead of cut glass. Unfortunately, English glassmakers cheapened the reputation of incrustations because of one more substitution. They made pressed items with intaglio-shaped pictures under the colorless glass and simply filled the hollows with plaster. From the other side these looked like the real glass incrustations. However, such glass pieces could be used only for sticking on other objects by some cold process; heat would destroy them.

CENTRAL EUROPE PRODUCTION

A solid fusion of glass with other materials, as is demonstrated by the many and varied metal mountings, has always been especially difficult. These difficulties will never be quite overcome. In spite of this, there have always been attempts to enclose some other materials into glass vessels, such as in the dice and coin glasses which were very much favored in the seventeenth and eighteenth century. (The oldest glass with an enclosed die, "v Ni Kostka Zadelana," is mentioned in 1584 in an interesting and detailed inventory of the collection of Lady Johanna Trzka von Leipa, which was in the archives in Wittingau.) The early glasses had only one die; later, in the first half of the eighteenth century, they usually had 3 dice. However, since these usually were made of bone, it was impossible to enclose the dice into red-hot glass. Therefore the die enclosure seems to be mostly done by the cold process, "Zwischengoldtechnik."

On the other hand, the coin glasses were produced by the hot process at the glassworks. Occasionally gold but usually silver coins were first welded together vertically and then placed into

Fig. I. Cameo necklace and matching earrings
by Apsley Pellatt. Collection of Mrs. Paul
Jokelson, Scarsdale, New York

Fig. II. (Upper Left) Brooch by Apsley Pellatt; Collection of Mrs. Paul Jokelson. (Lower Left) Cameo of Duc de Berry by Baccarat (?); Author's Collection. (Center) Tie pin by Apsley Pellatt; Collection of Mrs. Paul Jokelson. (Right) A pair of earrings by Apsley Pellatt; Collection of Florence Ackerman.

Fig. III. Baccarat. Private Collection, Paris, France

Figs. IV & V. (Facing page top left to right) Baccarat. Private Collection, Paris, France

Fig. VI. (Right) Unidentified medal and portrait of Sainte Clotilde by Baccarat. Author's Collection

Fig. VII. William Pitt by Apsley Pellatt, from a ceramic portrait by Leonard James Abington. Private Collection, Paris, France

Fig. VIII. Bohemian glass; 6″ high. Collection of Corning Museum of Glass, Corning, New York

Fig. IX. (Left) Bohemian glass with sulphide portrait of Goethe; Author's Collection. (Right) Pair of salts with sulphide portraits of Queen Victoria and the Duke of Wellington by Pellatt and Green (?); Private Collection, Paris, France

a plaque of circular shape called "Kodus-Zwischenglied," the border of which became pinched into a sharp edge, and later fitted into the bottom. (Coins imbedded in wall medallions or cups are seldom found.) This kind can be seen in gold on an old cut and gilt Potsdam cup of the Bayerische Gewerbeaustalt, which was in Nuremberg, and in silver on a richly cut Silesian cup of 1861, which is after the period of Biedermeier. Not all coins are solidly welded in; on the contrary, most of them sit inside the glass very loosely, can change their position, and can rattle.

In the case of incorporation of ceramic objects or "incrustations," this defect does not occur, because the porcelain of the sulphide is well bound with the soft crystal that surrounds it. The secret of success is primarily based on a very *precise* work. The ground work for this was laid by the efforts of collectors of jewels, jewel impressions, and jewel castings of all kinds.

During the Napoleonic era Germany could easily get glass incrustations from France for their dukes and famous people; therefore this technique spread to Germany, as well as to Austria, at a relatively late date. Because of the great lack of signatures, one cannot very well draw a sharp line, especially as the techniques and styles are so similar. Potsdam-Zechlin Glass Works were probably the first manufacturers of incrusted glass sulphides in Germany. The most important piece is the beautiful, polished egg-shaped vase in the Chateau on the Peacock Island which—according to the inventory of 1835—was given by the president of the Zechlin Glass Works to King Frederick William III (Fig. 10). The glass-incrusted reliefs or portraits of the royal couple and their seven living children were made after cast-iron medallions by L. Posch. They were put on a detachable band and are quite visible on the matt background between all the laurel leaves. Not only does the

previously mentioned inventory indicate Zechlin as the manufacturer, but the similarity of this sulphide to two other independent specimens, one in the museum of Gotha and one in
the collection of J. Muehsam in Berlin, which bear the engraved signatures "Zechnlinsche Gl. Heutte" and "Zechlin,"
would be further identification.

The incrusted portrait head of King Frederick William IV
is not uncommon; we often find the same head among those
already imitated. The bust portrait of his wife Elisabeth (after
a coin of Friedrich Loos-Berlin) is also in the form of an incrusted sulphide on a crystal vase in the Berlin Kunstgewerbe-
museum. Found also are the heads of other Berlin personages,
some of which must have been made in Zechlin. Of course this
glass factory, which at that time was under the management of
the government counselor, Metzger, made only utility glass.
At the Great Exhibitions in Berlin (1844) and in Munich
(1854) there was not one piece of this technique to be seen.

Where else glass incrustations were made in Germany is
difficult to determine today. Pictures of rulers, or coats of arms,
in the absence of signatures give very little to go on. The
octagonally incrusted sulphide of the first Würtemberg king,
Frederick (1816), once located in the castle Friedrichshafen,
certainly was not made in Würtemberg; also, the medallions
with the head of Frederick Augustus the Righteous were not
made in Saxony nor was a richly set seal with the bust of the
Saxon princess, formerly Spanish Queen Maria Josepha (1829).
The very frequent portrait incrustations of the Bavarian king
Max Josef I (1825), always without signature, certainly were
made in France or Bohemia, and in the many Bavarian glass-
works. The differences in the glasses used indicate various
origins. Portraits of Archduke Leopold of Baden (1790-1852),
and sometimes also of his wife Sophie, are incrusted in glass

Fig. 11. Emperor Francis I of Germany. Collection of Landes-Gewerbemuseum, Stuttgart, Germany

Fig. 10. Vase given by the president of the Zechlin Glass Works to King Frederick William III. The sulphides represent the royal couple and their seven children and were made from cast-iron medallions by L. Posch. *Present whereabouts unknown*

tumblers of rather heavy appearance, very seldom cut, just pressed after a medal by Kachel, who was a medallion maker and coin minter; they usually have a rather flat relief that is not good enough for French work.

Later in Old Austria we find examples of the art of incrustations, and then, of course, in Bohemia, the main glass-making region of the monarchy. Only since 1826 can these works be identified as products of the County of Harrach, the factory of Neuwelt in Riesengebirge on the frontier of Silesia. There the most exact glass sulphides were made in the 1830's. It is thus understandable that the steward of this glass works, Johann Pohl (March 22, 1850), let himself be painted by J. Gizel with a self-satisfied look, and holding an incrusted glass as well as a pen with which, at that time, gold ornaments were painted for the first time on the glasses of the Biedermeier period. Glass incrustations were shown for the first time at the Prague Industrial Exhibition of 1829, and with such great success they received the Gold Medal. The principal piece was a crystal set for sugared water, composed of a water bottle with an incrusted picture of Schiller in the stopper, of an arakbouteille with Mozart, and a sugar bowl with Goethe. Connecting Goethe with sweetness, or Mozart with spirits, must look as strange as the watering down of Schiller. In those days one wanted evidently to have, even during a drink, the company of one's favorite poet or composer and one believed that this strange "honor" would not hurt them. Goethe, who was still alive, does not seem to have protested, or at least there is no knowledge of such a protest. During this exhibition Neuwelt does not show just glass vessels but also "Postamente" of crystal with incrusted sulphides either as religious articles, such as a crucifix or a madonna, or as patriotic ornaments, such as a "column with a bust of the Emperor." More perfect are the crystal cups with the bust of Emperor Francis in the

Landesgewebermuseum in Stuttgart. Also there we find the portrait of the Duke of Reichstadt or the Duke of Nassau on a bottle or in a ruby cased glass. The picture of a mother with child and a madonna medallion are to be found on blue cased glasses.

We must, however, make a generalized division of the works between one or the other production place. Many French works were exported to Germany and Austria in the first thirty years of the nineteenth century. Therefore, most of the porcelain cups with the incrusted glass bottoms, medallions with the double portraits of Voltaire and Rousseau, the gold box with the incrusted Poniatowski (1813), at one time in the Shutchukin collection in the historical museum in Moscow, and other similar works have to be credited to France. The majority of the incrustations in English and American collections must be credited mostly to England. Of German origin, on the other hand, will be the pictures of Goethe or of Luther, or cut glasses that not only show, in the same technique, such celebrated Germans as Schiller, but also have old German mountings.

Enameled metal enclosures (usually gold enamel in glass)—as against enclosed coins—must be usually of French or English origin, even if, because of the subject, they would point in some other direction. In this technique we find represented most often the Legion of Honor and other medals. Flowers and emblems, however, are not rare. (Fig. III through VI.)

Imitations, as already mentioned, made the group of incrusted glasses seem less fine and cheapened them, and thus made them lose their popularity. Ordinary pressing replaced the earlier careful and tasteful cutting, and glass sulphides with or without plaster filling replaced the sulphides of incrusted porcelain bisque.

We have been unsuccessful in tracing some of the sulphides

reproduced in Pazaurek's book, since we received no answer to our letters to museums in Hamburg, Hanover, Stuttgart, and in what is now Czechoslovakia. We have reproduced two of the illustrations directly from Pazaurek's book, Figs. 10 and 11.

GREAT FRENCH CREATORS OF SULPHIDES

In Agen, we were very fortunate to meet Mademoiselle Anne-Marie Labit, curator of the Agen Museum, who showed us a number of sulphides given to the Museum by the Chevalier de Saint-Amans when he returned to France from England. Several of these magnificent pieces are pictured here together with the unique pictures, we believe, of de Saint-Amans and his father. These prints were found by Mademoiselle Labit in the archives of the Museum. (Figs. 12 and 13.)

Doctor Charles Lasserre, a distinguished physician from Bordeaux, France, and a great scholar of ceramics, has made a comprehensive study of the life and work of Saint-Amans. On November 12, 1967, with the collaboration of Mademoiselle Labit, he gave a lecture to the Société Archéologique de Bordeaux, under the title: "A curious episode in the life of the great Gascon ceramist, the Chevalier Honoré Boudon de Saint-Amans: the incrustations in crystal at the Agen Museum." With Doctor Lasserre's and Mademoiselle Labit's kind permission we are happy to share with you this most important information.

The Chevalier de Saint-Amans (Pierre Honoré Boudon de Saint-Amans), who is mentioned by Apsley Pellatt in *Curiosities of Glass-Making* (1849), was born May 9, 1774 in his father's castle of Saint-Amans, Commune of Castelculier. In

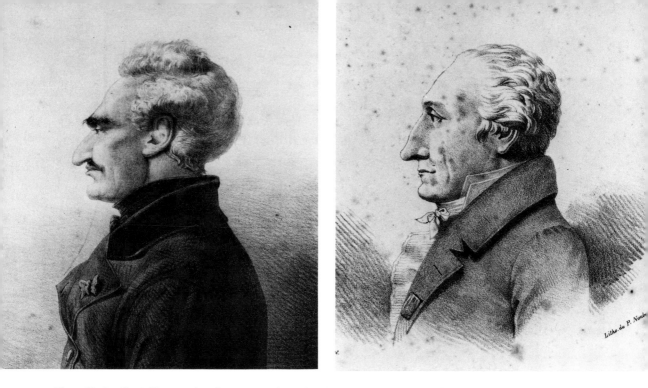

Figs. 12 & 13. Self-portrait of Honoré de Saint-Amans (*Left*). Portrait by Boudon de Saint-Amans (*Right*) of his father Florimond Boudon de Saint-Amans. *Collection of Agen Museum*

Figs. 14 & 15. Reproductions of patents for the making of flat medallions granted to Boudon de Saint-Amans.

1818 he took out a patent for making flat medallions, which is now preserved in the archives of the Conservatoire National des Arts et Métiers in Paris; a patent not for "inventing" but for "perfecting" the process of incrustating cameos in glass, thus presupposing that there was an earlier patent granted for the making of these little works of art. (Figs. 14 and 15.)

The following lines are quoted from a report on china decoration, published in 1850 at Agen. "If the idea of making

Fig. 16. "Motherhood" by Boudon de Saint-Amans. *Collection of Musée National de Céramique de Sèvres, France*

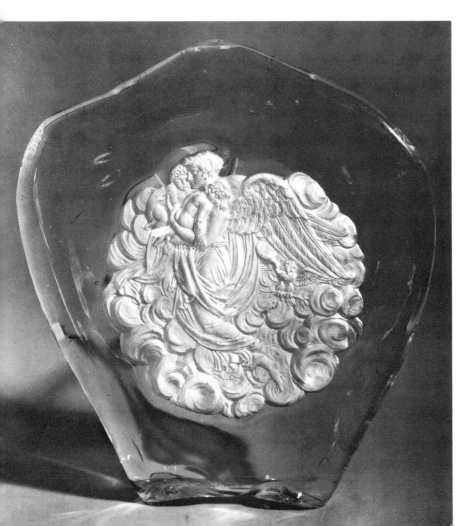

Fig. 17. Unidentified figure by Boudon
de Saint-Amans. (Twice actual size)
Collection of Agen Museum

cameos incrustated in crystal did not originate with him [Saint-Amans], he has at least left his name on this splendid industry, in raising it from its mediocre state, to produce marvels of artistic beauty, for which crowned heads paid by their weight in gold."

His stormy youth came during the period of the Revolution and it is said he nearly fell into the hands of the revolutionary tribunal, and later was nearly captured by the army of the revolutionary general, Hoche. Finally he found refuge in England, where he busied himself with ceramic work. Only after the Bourbon restoration did he return to his country, and in 1818 he got a position at the Sèvres porcelain works where he was active off and on between 1818 and 1826. From 1824 to 1827 he was also sometimes in Creil working as a ceramic artist. In 1836 Saint-Amans joined Johnston in order to estab-

Figs. 18 & 19. (Left) Duchesse d'Angoulême. *(Right)* Unidentified figure by Boudon de Saint-Amans. *Collection of Agen Museum*

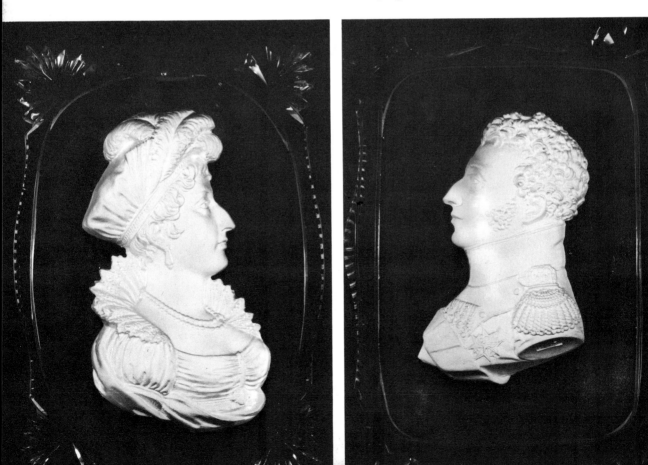

Fig. 20. François I, King of France, by Boudon de Saint-Amans. *Collection of Agen Museum*

Fig. 21. Allegorical figures by Boudon de Saint-Amans. *Collection of Agen Museum*

Fig. 22. Voltaire and Rousseau by Boudon de Saint-Amans. *Collection of Agen Museum*

Figs. 23 & 24. Crystal flask (*Left*) with a sulphide of Shakespeare by Boudon de Saint-Amans. *Collection of Musée des Arts Décoratifs, Paris, France.* Benjamin Franklin (*Right*) by Boudon de Saint-Amans. *Collection of Agen Museum*

lish an independent porcelain factory in Bordeaux. Later he founded one more factory, in Lamarque, which he managed until his death on March 14, 1858, from his chateau at Lamarque.

In order to protect himself against any possible competition and to enable him to sell his patent advantageously, he sold the rights to the royal crystal works in Mont-Cenis (near Creusot, Saone-et-Loire). This factory was especially interested in sulphides under Ladouepe-du-Fougerais and under the Brothers Chagot. They sold large quantities of these objects through their Paris branches (No. 10, rue de Bondy, and No. 11, Boulevard Poissonière), and some of the incrusted sulphides were even marked with "Brevet de Perfectionnement, Mre. Royale de Montcenis." Emperauger, who mentions two pieces signed in this way, does not know of any with the signature of Saint-Amans. The two pieces so marked are a head of Czar Alexander I of Russia, after an Andrieu medal of 1814 (Fig. 34), and a ring with the likeness of the Duc de Berry, after a medal by Gaynard. Other works by Saint-Amans, but not personally signed by him, some with colored incrustations, are at the Manufacture Nationale de Sèvres.

In the Museum of Sèvres also stands a cut glass column which has, on the center part of each side, a bombus-shaped, Wedgwood-like relief, with feminine allegorical figures, said to be a Paris work of 1796. More reliable is the date of 1798 found on two more pieces of the same collection, the circle-shaped bottom of tumblers with incorporated busts of Franklin and Voltaire, and a third one from the middle of the nineteenth century with the bust of Rousseau. They are signed "P. B. 1798" and they originated from the factory of H. B. Boileau in Gros-Caillou near Paris. This is the first identifiable place that made incrustations in modest quantities.

From what is known of Saint-Amans' life, it is likely that he soon stopped working at the Cristallerie de Mont-Cenis in order to devote his time once again to ceramics. In any case he was, for a time, one of the leaders among these highly skilled artisans who, at the beginning of the nineteenth century, practised the art of embedding glass and crystal. (Figs. 16 through 30; Figs. X through XII.)

The signature most often found on the finest sulphides is that of Desprez, of whom even his countrymen still know very little, not even his first name, or dates of his birth or death. He and Leconte were the top chemists of the Manufacture Nationale de Sèvres during the year 1773. He may already have been concerned not only with the pure scientific and practical questions, but also with the esthetics. By 1780 he was known as "sculpteur de première classe." In 1793 he settled as an independent manufacturer at No. 2, rue des Recollets, and he appeared as such in the Paris Commercial Almanac of 1807, 1812, and 1813, chiefly as a producer of porcelain cameos, which had such a success at the Paris Exhibition of 1806 that he was given the silver medal of second class. They were used in jewelry and for the decorating of china vases. There is mention of his elegant china cups, but no mention of glass incrustations. During the Louvre Exhibition of 1819 where Saint-Amans, who was not present at the 1806 exhibition, was

Fig. 25. A pair of crystal flasks incrusted with sulphides by Boudon de Saint-Amans. *Collection of Musée des Arts Décoratifs, Paris, France*

Figs. 26 & 27. Plaques by Boudon de Saint-Amans. *Collection of Agen Museum*

Fig. 28. Plaque by Boudon de Saint-Amans. *Collection of Agen Museum*

Fig. 29. Flask by Boudon de Saint-Amans. (Twice actual size) *Collection of Agen Museum*

Fig. 30. Plaque by Boudon de Saint-Amans. *Collection of Agen Museum*

expressly mentioned as maker of incrusted sulphides, Desprez appeared only as the maker of porcelain cameos. He still lived in the rue des Recollets, although in 1798 there is a note of an address in rue de Lancry, where perhaps his laboratory was adjacent to the store. After 1815 Desprez, the father, is no longer mentioned. On the other hand, after the Exhibition of 1819 his son's name (again, the first name is not known) appeared in the Commercial Almanac under the same address, No. 2, rue des Recollets-du-Temple, as the maker of porcelain cameos in the Wedgwood style and of equipment for painting and gilding of china. For the first time his name appeared with the description, "Assortement de Médailles dans l'intérieur de cristal," which had never been mentioned with the name of his father.

The son worked first in porcelain for which he received a five-year casting patent for the porcelain sulphide that he invented (from Nevers sand, white quartz, purified kaolin from Limoges, and earth from Dreux). He received another patent for an enamel composition (from Nevers and white sand, then sand earth of Nevers and white Spanish chalk, in equal ratios). The rest of the sulphide patent describes the careful cleaning process (especially from traces of iron) and the mixing of the materials, as well as the most important advantage of its fire-proof quality. According to the Paris Almanacs of 1821 and 1823, he switched completely to the incrustation of sulphides in glass. He is mentioned as having these in stock as room ornaments—framed in bronze or at least with a hook for hanging on the walls—or as part of bottles, candy jars, religious objects, and jewelry settings. Medallions with busts of rulers are specially mentioned. In 1825 he moved to No. 23, rue des Morts (near the Faubourg St. Martin) and in 1829 into rue St. Jacques, his last address until 1830, whereupon all trace of him is lost.

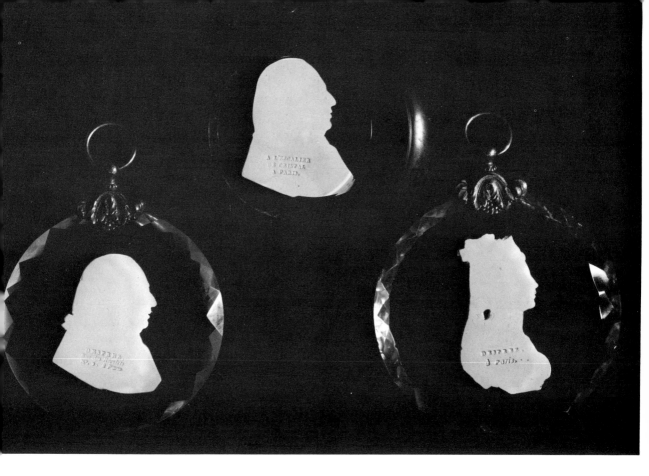

Fig. 31. Various signatures on the backs of sulphides: "à l'Escalier de cristal, à Paris" is imprinted on the reverse of a white clay profile of Louis XVIII; Desprez used five different signatures of which two are shown here. *Author's collection*

Fig. 32. Empress Josephine by Desprez imprinted with the signature "Desprez, à Paris." *Private Collection, Paris, France*

Fig. 33. "The Agony in the
Garden" by Desprez.
Author's Collection

Fig. 34. A head of Czar Alexander I
of Russia by Desprez, after an
Andrieu medal of 1814; an identical
sulphide is impressed "Montcenis" on
the back. *Author's Collection*

The actual work itself discloses the existence of the Desprez sulphides incrusted in glass before the known historical sources, which speak about them only in 1819. It is certain that Desprez, Jr., and perhaps his father before him (during the reign of Napoleon I), had not only mastered the technique of incrustation, but did so with a perfection that his contemporaries or his successors seldom achieved. There are five different signatures which were made on the back of the sulphides (Fig. 31) with a dry stamp. Their chronological order is not known:

1. D.P., larger letters
2. D.P., smaller letters
3. DESPREZ
4. DESPREZ
   à Paris
5. DESPREZ
   Rue des Recolets   (always in 3 lines and with
   No. 2 à Paris   one "1" in "Recolets")

These markings had already been noted on the reverse of embedded cameos by the Count de Chavagnac and the Marquis de Grollier, who listed them on page 628 of their *Histoire des Manufactures Françaises de Porcelaine* (published in France in 1906).

All of Desprez's sulphides are conspicuous for their great precision. Neither do they show air lines or air pockets nor the small bubbles which so often are visible near the sulphide rim, especially near the nose and chin, in the work of his later imitators. Desprez seems to have destroyed poorly made pieces and never to have allowed them to be sold. The minuscule

Figs. 35 & 36. Napoleon I and Marie-Louise (*Left*) by Desprez, from a medal by Andrieu. Napoleon I (*Right*), by Desprez, after a die by Andrieu. *Collection of Musée des Arts Décoratifs, Paris, France*

air particles, which stayed inside the mass of bisque of the sulphide after a good drying and firing process, came out after incrustation into the glass and pressed themselves between the glass and the sulphide. This caused a thin film which ordinarily acquired a silvery sheen. The careful cutting of both sides, the round bevel on the medallions which sometimes have dia-

Fig. 37. (*Upper Left*) King of Rome. (*Lower Right*) Empress Marie-Louise by
Desprez. *Author's Collection*

Fig. 38. (*Left*) Duchesse d'Angoulême. (*Right*) Duchesse de Berry by Desprez.
Author's Collection

Fig. 39. Henry IV, King of France, by Desprez. *Private Collection, Paris, France*

mond cutting on the back, and a mounting in gilt bronze, all contributed to the fact that these artworks found the favor of a high-class public, who spread them in all directions as the finest souvenirs from Paris. Desprez knew how to impress his international clientele when he included in his collection the various potentates with their families, usually in the form of decorative hanging medallions, candy-boxes, paperweights, decanters, or the bottoms of porcelain cups in Empire style.

The commerce in these objects was widespread and there existed a large number of manufacturers and dealers—here are the most important, with the markings and monograms they used:

Desprez, No. 2, rue des Recollets, Paris

Imprinted on the reverse of steatite cameo profiles representing: 1) Napoleon, after a die by Andrieu (Fig. 36), which was used in Paris as early as 1804 for the heads of several medals having different backs; 2) the joined profiles of Napoleon and Marie-Louise, after a die by Andrieu (Fig. 35), used to strike a medal commemorating the wedding of the Emperor and Marie-Louise and a second medal at the birth of the king of Rome; 3) the Duchesse de Berry, the Duchesse d'Angoulême, Louis XVIII, and Henry IV (Figs. 38, 39, and 61).

All these cameos are incrusted within circular crystal medallions, which were generally richly framed or held in gilt-bronze settings.

D.P., D.P.

Desprez's monogram, in two sizes (Fig. 40). Imprinted on the reverse of four cameos. One of these represents Mars and Venus, with the slightly idealized features of Murat and his wife Caroline Bonaparte (Fig. 41). Murat is wearing a Roman helmet surmounted by a lion in a reclining position. This outstandingly beautiful cameo seems to be the original work of Desprez, and bears a striking resemblance to the wax model executed on December 31, 1810, or a certain one-sided medal, which once formed a part of the Depaulis collection. This item had been prepared by Gayrard, who intended to produce a cameo bearing the joined

Fig. 40. Various signatures on the backs of cameos. (*Top*) D.P. and Dihl. (*Bottom*) Montcenis and Schmidt.

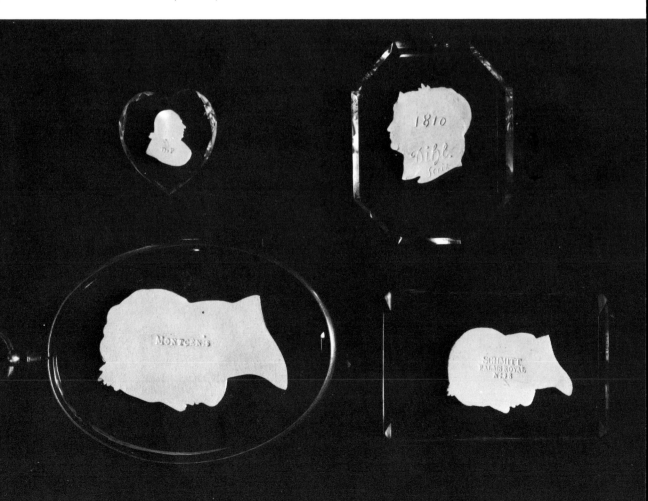

Figs. 41 & 42. Prince Murat and his wife Caroline (*Left*) *Private Collection, Paris, France.* Duc de Berry (*Right*) by Desprez. *Collection of the Musée Condé, Chantilly, France*

Fig. 43. Pope Pius IX by Desprez. *Private Collection, Paris, France*

Figs. 44 & 45. Duchesse d'Angoulême *(Left).* Duchesse de Berry *(Right)* by Acloque. *Collection of Musée des Arts Décoratifs, Bordeaux, France*

heads of the Emperor and Marie-Louise. The other cameos carry the likenesses of the Duc de Berry (Fig. 42), and Pope Pius VII (Fig. 43).

Acloque, fils, No. 22, rue de la Barillerie, Paris

Imprinted on the reverse of a white clay profile of Louis XVIII, incrusted in a round crystal medallion, set in a frame of the period. The rue de la Barillerie disappeared during the reign of Napoleon III and became the much wider

Boulevard du Palais. It was occupied by leading merchants. The kings and their household often followed this street to and from the Louvre and Notre-Dame. Under Louis XVIII, on Corpus-Christi Day, a temporary altar was built there and Count d'Artois, the Duchesse d'Angoulême, and the Duchesse de Berry stopped at this altar. (Figs. 44 and 45).

Acloque, Jr., as a successor to his father, operated a large shop at the same location from 1815 to 1830. This shop sold "glass, crystal and earthenware, as well as everything required for Physics and Chemistry." In 1833 he sold his establishment to Messrs. Vimeux and Cocheteux.

C.A.

Letters traced in red on the reverse of two steatite cameos representing William I and William II, kings of the Netherlands, inlaid within crystal flasks (Figs. 46 and 47. See also Fig. 77).

Figs. 46 & 47. Steatite cameo of William I of Orange (*Left*) with a crystal flask. Steatite cameo of William II of Orange (*Right*) within a crystal flask by Cattaert. *Private Collection, Paris, France*

These two letters no doubt constitute the monogram of the Cattaert family, listed in the Commercial Almanacs, from 1815 through the reign of Louis Philippe, among the crystal manufacturers and decorators. It is also reported that this family produced incrusted objects. Their address was No. 6, rue Mandar, then No. 25, Faubourg Saint-Denis.

Compagnie des Cristalleries de Baccarat

A certain M. Dartigues prepared crystals for the widowed Mme. Desarnaud-Charpentier who, between 1802 and 1828, owned the Escalier de Cristal in Paris. These crystals were then finished at Mme. Desarnaud's workshop. Some of them contained incrusted cameos. Dartigues was a remarkable glassmaker who, during the Empire, was the director of crystal-works situated in Paris, at No. 64, rue du Mont-Blanc or No. 30, Faubourg Poissonière. During the same period, he also founded the Vorrêche crystal-works, which he then moved to Baccarat, after the treaties of 1814 changed the French frontier-line and left Vorrêche under foreign domination.

Fig. 48. Paperweight, "The Hunter" by Baccarat. *Collection of The John Nelson Bergstrom Museum and Art Center, Neenah, Wisconsin*

It was thus likely that the Baccarat crystal-works had produced sulphides, not only under the directorship of Dartigues, but also under the first few of his successors. This is definitely established by the existence, in the Conservatoire National des Arts et Métiers, of three items given to that Museum in 1851 by the Cristalleries de Baccarat:

1) No. 6048 in the Museum Catalog: a crystal column surmounted by a crystal cross, with a white clay Virgin.

2) No. 6094: a crystal paperweight, with white clay hunting scene. (Fig. 50. This is similar to a weight in the John Nelson Bergstrom Museum, Neenah, Wisconsin Fig. 48.)

3) No. 6080: another crystal paperweight, with an imagiary head, in white clay.

Of all the establishments manufacturing sulphides, the Cristalleries de Baccarat is probably the one which remained active in this field for the longest period of time. See the history of Baccarat, pages 75-95.

Dihl

Dihl, whose name is well known from the history of the Paris Empire porcelains (Fig. 40), was one of the better Parisian representatives of glass incrustation art. His full name is to be found on a medallion of octagonal shape with the head of Napoleon and Marie Louise (Fig. 51). Dihl and Guerard were, in fact, the agents of the private factory of the Duc d'Augoulême, rue de Bondy.

l'Escalier de Cristal, Paris

Imprinted: 1) on the reverse of a white clay profile of Louis XVIII, after the medal engraved by Andrieu in 1817, incrusted in a circular crystal medal (Fig. 31); 2) on the reverse of two identical white clay likenesses of the Holy Virgin, incrusted in the branches of a magnificent pair of candlesticks, 29 centimeters high, made of richly cut crystal.

The cameos sold by the Escalier de Cristal, although they carried the markings of this establishment, originated from the Dartigues factory which was founded under the Empire, at No. 64, rue du Mont-Blanc.

Fabrique de Cristal à Paris

Traced in red on the reverse of a steatite cameo representing Henry IV, after Droz in a small circular medallion, which in turn is encased in the center of the lid of a cut crystal jewel-case.

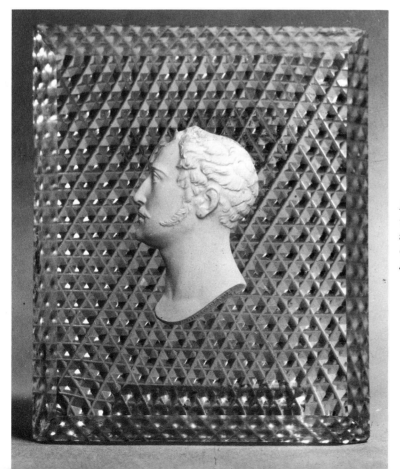

Fig. 49. Incrusted cameo of the head of Czar Nicholas I, after a medal by Nicolesko. *Collection of Musée de Sèvres, France*

Fig. X. Two paperweights by Saint-Amans. Collection of Agen Museum

Fig. XI: By Saint-Amans. Collection of Agen Museum

Fig. XII. Two plaques by Saint-Amans; the label reads: "Baked argillaceous clay printed with vitrifiable colors incrusted in crystal at Creusot, near Mont-Cenis (Saone and Loire) by M. de Saint-Amans, in July 1829. Exhibit of 1819. Given by M. de Saint-Amans." Collection of Musée National de Céramique de Sèvres, France

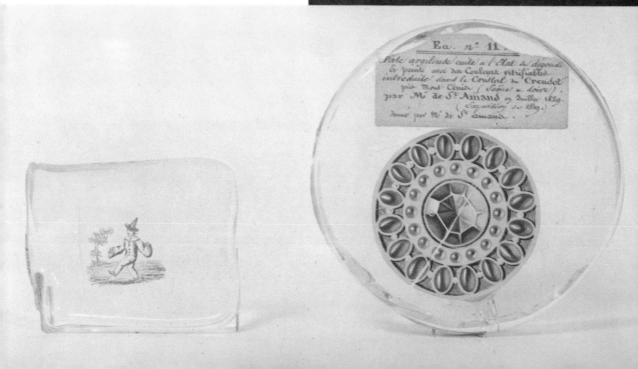

Fig. XIII. Paris cabinet cup and saucer; the cup has a glass base containing a cameo of Napoleon, after Andrieu, and is impressed with the signature "Desprez, Rue des Recolets, No. 2, à Paris." Author's Collection

Fig. XIV. Porcelain cup and saucer (probably Sèvres); sulphide of unknown person, perhaps Lafayette. Collection of The John Nelson Bergstrom Art Center and Museum, Neenah, Wisconsin

Fig. XV. Profile of Queen Victoria in
overlay paperweight by Baccarat.
Collection of The New York Historical
Society, New York, New York

Fig. XVI. Figure of Joan of Arc in tumbler
by Baccarat. Private Collection, Paris,
France

Fig. XVII. Profile of George Washington,
after Duvivier, by Baccarat. Collection
of The John Nelson Bergstrom Museum
and Art Center, Neenah, Wisconsin

Fig. XVIII. (Upper Left) Saint Paul by Baccarat; Author's Collection. (Lower Left) Madame de Montespan by Baccarat; Author's Collection. (Upper Right) Duke of Wellington impressed with "à l'Escalier de Cristal, à Paris"; Collection of Paul Loraine, Esquire, London, England. (Lower Right) Opaline box with allegoric sulphide by Baccarat; Author's Collection

Fig. XIX. Unidentified profile by Baccarat (?). Collection of The John Nelson Bergstrom Museum and Art Center, Neenah, Wisconsin

Feuillet, No. 20, rue de la Paix à Paris

Imprinted on the reverse side of a white cameo representing the Duchesse d'Angoulême in an uncut crystal medallion. Judging from various striking points of resemblance which have established, this is certainly the work of the manufacturer Desprez. From contemporary Commercial Almanacs, this Feuillet was a fashionable porcelain-maker who, as early as 1816, called himself "Patented by the Prince de Condé and the Duc de la Paix." In 1820 he moved from No. 20 to No. 18 of the rue de la Paix. His firm, in various hands, remained in existence for a very long period of time.

La Villette

The glass works of La Villette, outside Paris, produced the incrusted cameo with the head of the Russian Czar Nicholas I, now at the Sèvres Museum (Fig.49).

Fig. 50. Saint Charles Borromeo by Martoret. *Author's Collection*

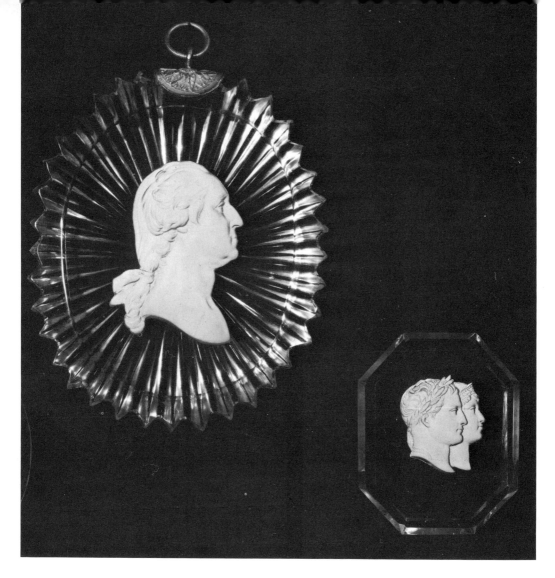

Fig. 51. (Upper Left) A white clay cameo of George Washington by Martoret, from the medal by Duvivier pictured below it. *(Lower Right)* The joined heads of Napoleon and Marie-Louise, from the medal by Andrieu pictured below it; signed "Dihl-Paris." *Author's Collection*

Fig. 52. Tumbler containing white clay profile of the Duc de Bordeaux as a child by Martoret, after the engraver Dubois. *Collection of Musée des Arts Décoratifs, Paris, France*

Martoret, Paris manufacturer of "crystal medals."

Starting in 1823, Martoret, a manufacturer of incrusted cameos, is listed in the Paris Commercial Almanacs as "Manufacturer of crystal medals." Among his works we find: A superb elliptical medallion of cut crystal, with gilt-bronze setting, in which is a white clay cameo of Washington, after Duvivier (Fig. 51); a very fine cut crystal medallion con-

Fig. 53. A plaque by Martoret with the joined profiles of Voltaire and Rousseau, after a medal engraved by Caunois. *Author's Collection*

taining a cameo of Saint Charles Borromeo (Fig. 50); a tumbler, containing the white clay profile of the Duc de Bordeaux (Fig. 52), after the engraver Dubois; and a plaque with the joined profiles of Voltaire and Rousseau, after a medal engraved by Caunois in 1818. (Fig. 53).

"Mont-Cenis" and "Brevet de Perfectionnement Mre. Royale de Mont-Cenis"

One of these markings is imprinted on the reverse of a steatite cameo representing the profile of Alexander I, Emperor of Russia, after the medal engraved by Andrieu in 1814. This cameo (Fig. 40) is embedded within an elliptical crystal medallion. The other marking is imprinted on the reverse of the cameo representing the Duc de Berry, after Gayrard, and placed in the center of a richly cut circular crystal medallion set in a clapper-ring.

Paris, Joaillier, Bijoutier et Orfèvre, à Paris.

Paris, whose address was No. 13, rue Croix-des-Petits-Champs, in Paris, was also a manufacturer of sulphides. Like Desprez, he presented some of his work at the 1819 Exhibition and was awarded an honorable mention.

P.B. 1798

Markings traced by stylus on the reverse of a terracotta cameo of Franklin in a round crystal medal. This cameo is well executed and seems to be an original work (Fig. 54). The initials are those of Boileau, whose widow presented these sulphides to the Sèvres Museum in 1845.

Sage à la Gard

Stylus-traced on the reverse of a white clay cameo bearing the profile of Louis XVIII, in the center of a circular crystal medal, which in turn is set in a black wooden frame of the Restoration style; we know nothing about Sage.

Fig. 54. "P.B. 1798" is traced with a stylus on the reverse of this terracotta cameo of Franklin. The initials are those of Boileau. *Collection of Musée National de Céramique de Sèvres, France*

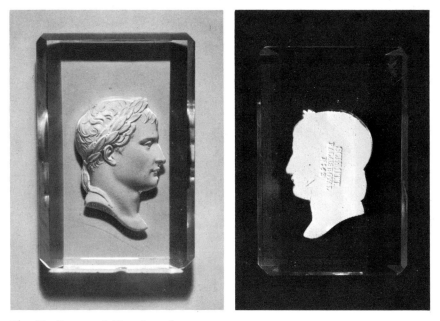

Fig. 55. Cameo of Napoleon by Schmitt. *Collection of Florence Ackerman*

Schmitt, No. 43, Palais-Royal

Early in the nineteenth century, Schmitt was listed in the Commercial Almanacs among the crystal dealers. His complete address was: "Schmitt (J. B.), Palais-Royal, Galerie de Pierre, 43." He was mentioned for the first time in 1813. His shop was in the Palais-Royal and his storehouse on the rue du Mail. He had disappeared by the year 1830. (Figs. 40 and 55).

The manufacturers had their own warehouses and shops, and sold some of their products directly. They also worked against orders placed by the leading dealers. In the latter case,

Fig. 56. Two flasks incrusted with profiles of Napoleon I by Baccarat, from the medal by Andrieu. *Collection of Musée des Arts Décoratifs, Paris, France*

they sometimes traced the name and address of the dealer on the reverse of the cameo before covering it with crystal.

Without exception, the principal dealers were situated on streets where wealthy strollers congregated: rue de la Barillerie, Palais-Royal, rue de la Paix. From this we conclude that incrusted cameos, portraits, and crystal medals were considered—at least during the Restoration—as highly fashionable and luxurious wares.

Another indication of the esteem these sulphides enjoyed at the time is found in an article by M. Charvet, a former architect in Lyons, on the medals and tokens in that city. This article is included in issue No. 227 (year 1908) of the *Gazette Numismatique Française*. On page 22 it is stated that in 1821, under the reign of Louis XVIII, when the equestrian statue of Louis XIV was rebuilt in Lyons' Place Bellecour, a lead box was placed in the foundation stone of the monument and contained, among other objects, "several crystal portraits of Louis XIV and one of the Duc d'Angoulême."

Sulphides played an important part in the political propaganda, creating either a favorable or hostile climate for the Empire, the Monarchy, and the party of liberty. In the Medal Gallery, in the Musée Carnavalet, there are 29 medals and coins of the Premier Empire which were placed by Napoleon in the cornerstone of the old "Cour des Comptes" destroyed during the "Commune" on April 4, 1810. These pieces were rediscovered on January 4, 1899, during the excavation for the construction of the Gare du Quai d'Orsay. Among these medals there are three sulphides. They represent Napoleon in profile, two with the crown of laurels, after Andrieu (Fig. 56), and the third one, without a crown, larger and superb, after Gallé.

These were documents of a new genre which prove that Napoleon highly regarded the art of "sulphide," which had been the object of notable exhibitions in Paris.

One question remains: Were the manufacturers of incrusted cameos merely skillful artisans, or were they real artists?

The truth is that these manufacturers fell into both categories. The majority, perhaps, were highly skilled artisans— they molded cameos from a variety of relief objects, and mainly from medals executed by contemporary engravers. Occasionally they also copied biscuit medallions of the Manufacture de Sèvres.

However, some of the cameo manufacturers were also excellent artists and have left small masterpieces that show real originality and creative imagination.

It is therefore clear that the manufacture of incrusted cameos certainly constituted a genuine form of art, particularly when they were carried out by sculptors such as the two Desprez, by talented inventors such as the Chevalier de Saint-Amans, by jewelers such as Paris, and by crystal-works such as Baccarat, the establishment owned by Dartigues, Clichy, Mont-Cenis, and Saint Louis in France; in England by Pellatt and Green; in Scotland by John Ford and Company.

There is no doubt that this manufacture was artistic, brilliant, and luxurious.

SULPHIDE MARBLES AND CZECHOSLOVAKIAN SULPHIDE PAPERWEIGHTS

We are indebted for the following information to Mrs. Barbara Bowles Sisson, who has a comprehensive collection of these objects.

"Very little is known about when or where sulphide marbles were made. The technique was similar to that used in making sulphide paperweights. All research seems to indicate, though, that they were made between the years of 1878 and 1926 in both Germany and the United States. It seems impossible, at present, to determine which ones were made at what time or even in what sections of these countries.

"A few facts about these marbles seem apparent. The workmanship is poor. They are frequently found with large bubbles encasing part or all of the sulphide, cracks in the sulphide, pieces of the sulphide missing, poor coloring of the glass, and other imperfections. It seems that production was very small

Fig. 57. Paperweight containing a sulphide of an eagle. *Collection of Barbara Bowles Sisson*

because accumulating a collection of any size takes time and diligent searching. Yet, they were made in a surprising number of subjects that would appeal to children: dogs, cats, bears, lions, elephants, porcupines, fish, lizards, monkeys, rabbits, squirrels, children, foxes, wolves, sheep, pigs, cows, chickens, other poultry, birds, angels, Roman numerals, arabic numbers, horses, and so on. There are also many variations of the same figure. For example, there are many breeds of dogs and dogs in many different positions. Most of these sulphides are white. It is rare, indeed, to find a marble with a touch of color in the sulphide.

"Many questions about manufacture still exist, but there is little question that they were enjoyed by the children who owned them. From the number of bangs they received, they must have been for play and not just to be admired.

"It is known that sulphide paperweights were made in Czechoslovakia during its brief existence from 1918 to 1938.

Fig. 58. Sulphide marble. *Collection of Barbara Bowles Sisson*

Their sheen is different from that found in French sulphides, being more silvery; and the workmanship, while detailed, is not good. Also the casing glass leaves much to be desired.

"These sulphides have a three-dimensional quality similar to the ones found in marbles. Also the large bubbles found around the sulphides and the many small bubbles in the casing glass are present in the paperweights just as they are in the marbles. There seems to be a similarity of subject matter, too; but the sulphides in paperweights are much larger, more detailed, and different in color.

"The eagle illustrated here (Fig. 57) is sitting on a nest which contains two eggs. This nest rests on a cushion of tightly packed multi-color bits of glass and the crude swirls of glass surrounding this cushion are light green. The colored bases in other Czechoslovakian paperweights are similar. Many of these weights are nicely faceted."

Fig. 59. Finely wrought flat buttons with sulphide centers. *Collection of Mrs. George Ertell*

SULPHIDE BUTTONS

On the subject of sulphide buttons we quote from an article by our friend, the late George Ertell, published in the 1962 issue of the Paperweight Collectors' Association bulletin:

"Equally rare and comparable to the fine paperweights of the period are 'sulphide' buttons.

"Shown [in Fig. 59] are the finely wrought and larger types of the flat buttons with sulphide centers known to the collectors as 'Colonials.' The seven buttons with animal designs have blue painted waffle backgrounds. The button on the top of the picture is no doubt an example of the early experimental work of Apsley Pellatt. The design is from a painting of a Spanish setter by Stubbs. A scroll bearing the motto "Take Heed," is above the animal. The three buttons on the lower part of the plate are dull classical heads and allegorical subjects, definitely reversed intaglios, with plain dark blue painted backgrounds.

"It should be evident that these little gems constitute an undisputed form of art and deserve their recognition along with the creative glass of cameo incrustation."

W. RIDGWAY AND SON

The Ridgway family became interested in the potteries near the end of the eighteenth century. In 1792, Job Ridgway and his brother George acquired the Bell Bank Works at Hanley, Staffordshire. This partnership continued until 1802 when Job Ridgway established his own factory at Cauldon Place. His two sons, John and William, succeeded their uncle at the Bell Bank Works. John left to follow his father at the Cauldon Works in 1830 and William extended the Bell Bank factory.

Several other firms came under Ridgway ownership and the whole concern, known as W. Ridgway & Son, was finally dissolved in 1854. Shortly afterward the Bell Bank Works were purchased by Joseph Clementson.

All kinds of pottery and porcelain were made in the factories owned by the Ridgway family. The Ridgways also pioneered

Fig. 60. Portrait reliefs by Ridgway and Sons. Were exported to France for fusion into glass. (*From left to right, top to bottom*) John Wesley, William Pitt, William Shakespeare, George IV, Elizabeth Bonaparte, Joséphine Bonaparte, Louis XVI, Gassendi, Duchesse d'Angoulême, the royal family of Spain, and Lord Duncan. *Collection of Victoria and Albert Museum, London, England.*

73

several decorative processes, including the application of photography.

Leonard James Abington, born in 1785 and died in 1867, was a potter, designer, modeller, and a Baptist minister. He worked as carver and modeller for Benjamin Wyatt and Sir John Soane in London. He came to Hanley in 1819 and worked as modeller for Jacob Phillips and Joseph Mayer until 1831 when he entered into partnership with William Ridgway in the firm of Ridgway and Abington. The partnership was dissolved in 1860.

CRISTALLERIES
DE BACCARAT

Baccarat is a small town of about 6,000 people in Lorraine, about 250 miles due east of Paris, in the foothills of the Vosges Mountains. In 1764, when Monseigneur de Montmorency-Laval, Bishop of Metz, petitioned Louis XV, King of France, to allow him to set up a glassware factory across the Meurthe River from Baccarat, its population was barely 600. Why Baccarat and why a glassworks? Because the Bishop of Metz owned the land and the thousands of acres of woodland on it. Having lost most of the income from his forests due to the shutdown of a nearby salt factory, which had used his wood as fuel, he decided to set up some local industry that would require large amounts of wood and settled on glassmaking. Baccarat seemed an ideal location. The wood could be floated down to it, and the local population would furnish the manpower.

King Louis XV granted the charter, and in 1765 the Compagnie des Cristalleries de Baccarat was established. The

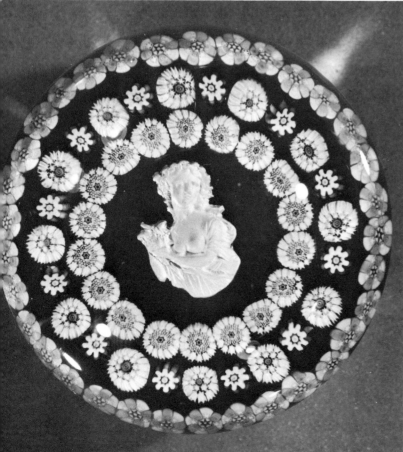

Fig. 61. (*Left to Right*) General
Foy and Napoleon I by
Baccarat. Louis XVIII signed
"Desprez." *Author's Collection*

Fig. 62. Paperweight by
Baccarat. *Collection of Musée
du Conservatoire National des
Arts et Métiers, Paris, France*

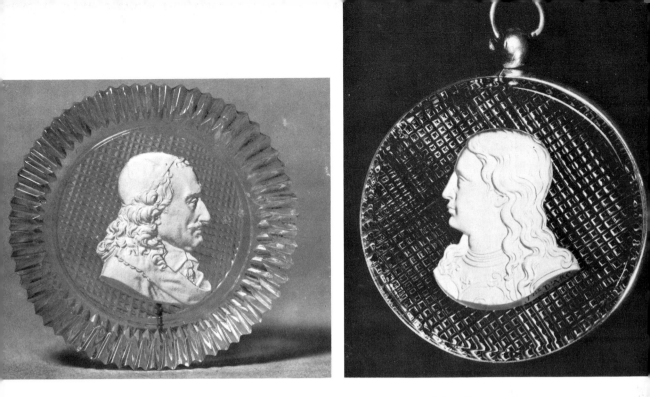

Figs. 63 & 64. Pierre Corneille (*Left*) by Baccarat, after a medal by E. Gatteaux. *Collection of Musée de Sèvres, France.* Joan of Arc (*Right*) by Baccarat. *Collection of Fred A. Nagel, Chicago, Illinois*

Fig. 65. Scent bottles. (*Left*) Napoleon I by Baccarat, after Andrieu. (*Right*) Louis XVI by Baccarat. *Author's Collection*

Figs. 66 & 67. Eugène de Beauharnais (*Left*) by Baccarat (?), after Franz Xaver Lösch. "Virgin and Child" (*Right*) by Baccarat. *Author's Collection*

Figs. 68 & 69. Czar Nicholas I of Russia (*Left*) by Baccarat. *Courtesy of Sotheby and Co., London, England*. George Washington (*Right*) by Baccarat, after Duvivier. *Collection of The Metropolitan Museum of New York, New York.*

Fig. 70. Pair of flasks by Baccarat. *Collection of Musée du Conservatoire National des Arts et Métiers, Paris, France*

79

Fig. 71. General Jackson, impressed with his name on back of sulphide. *Author's Collection*

Fig. 72. Water pitcher with the crest of Charles X by Baccarat. *Collection of Cristalleries de Baccarat Museum, Baccarat, France*

Fig. 73. French General B. D. H. Chassé by Baccarat. *Collection of Musée des Arts Décoratifs, Paris, France*

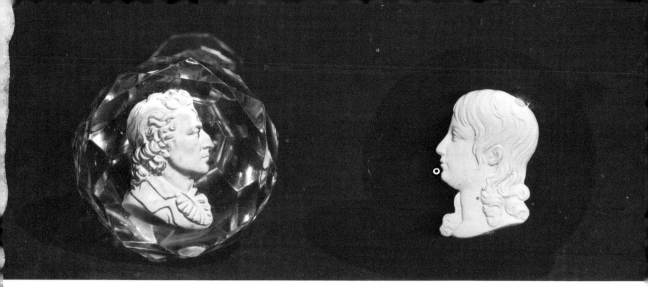

Fig. 74. (*Left*) Marie Joseph de Chenier. (*Right*) Louis XVII by Baccarat. *Author's Collection*

Fig. 75. (*Left*) Napoleon I in the uniform of Colonel of the Guard by Baccarat. (*Right*) Jesus Christ by Baccarat (?). *Author's Collection*

Fig. 76. Three-dimensional sculptures by Baccarat (?). *Author's Collection*

Bishop then found a financial backer, built a factory along the Meurthe River, and found a technician named Antoine Renaut to run it.

Business flourished so that at the time of the French Revolution the workers' force totaled 400. An interesting account of the time mentions that 70 workers' families were lodged in dwellings built by the factory, within its area. This was both a reflection of the management's early concern for the welfare of its employees and the result of practical necessity. At that time the melting of all the ingredients that went into glassmaking was very unpredictable and depended on various factors such as weather conditions, quality of the wood, and ability of the firemen. The molten "metal," as it is called, could be just right at any unpredictable time of the day or

Fig. 77. (*Upper Left*) Crystal cross
with Christ by Baccarat. (*Upper
Right*) Louis XVI, King of France;
marked "D.P." (Desprez). (*Bottom,
Left to Right*) William I, King of
the Netherlands, marked "C.A.";
President John Quincy Adams;
and Napoleon I, from a medal by
Desmarets, by Baccarat. *Author's
Collection*

Fig. 78. Louis Philippe, King of
France, by Baccarat. *Author's
Collection*

Fig. 79. Henry IV, King of France, by Baccarat; signed "E. Gatteaux, 1815." (Half actual size) *Author's Collection*

Fig. 80. Doorknob with sulphides of Presidents Harrison and Monroe by Baccarat (?). *Courtesy of Sotheby and Co., London, England*

Fig. 81. Tumbler with sulphide of Martin Luther by Baccarat. *Author's Collection*

Fig. 82. Jacques Delille, from the medal by Petit. *Collection of Musée des Arts Décoratifs, Paris, France*

Fig. 83. Charles X, after Gayrard, by Baccarat. *Author's Collection*

Fig. 84. Poquelin de Molière by Baccarat, from a medal by Gayrard. *Collection of Musée des Arts Décoratifs, Paris France*

Fig. 85. Flasks by Baccarat. *Collection of Musée des Arts Décoratifs, Paris, France*

Figs. 86 & 87. (Left) French actor Talma by Baccarat, from the medal by Caunois. *(Right)* Napoleon I, Marie-Louise, and the King of Rome by Baccarat, from a medal by Andrieu. *Collection of Musée des Arts Décoratifs, Paris, France*

night. It was therefore essential that the workers live nearby.

Production during these first successful years was varied but not fancy: regular glassware, mirror-glass, window-glass, bottles.

The French Revolution, which started in 1789, was the first blow that hurt Baccarat. Then came the Napoleonic Wars. Prices soared, orders became rare, and the labor force fell to below 70. In 1816 the factory was sold for 2,845 ounces of fine gold ($99,575). The purchaser, Monsieur d'Artigues, a Belgian, was an expert in the field as he owned and operated

Fig. 88. (Left) Queen Marie Antoinette of France by Baccarat, from a medal by Duvivier (?). *(Right)* King Louis XVI of France by Baccarat, from a medal by J. P. Droz (?). *Collection of Musée des Arts Décoratifs, Paris, France*

the glass factory of Vonêche in Belgium. He immediately decided to aim at prestige and to concentrate only on the production of full-lead crystal. Baccarat was never to depart from that all-important decision.

From 1817 to this day Baccarat has made nothing but full-lead crystal and has endlessly searched for better ways of producing the finest. In so doing it has contributed several new techniques to the field of crystalmaking. By the middle of the nineteenth century Baccarat had created entirely new com-

Fig. XX. (Left) Henry IV
by Boudon de Saint-Amans.
(Right) Napoleon I by
Baccarat. Author's Collection

Fig. XXI. Napoleon I in the
uniform of Colonel of the
Guard, after Andrieu. Private
Collection, Paris, France

Fig. XXII. Esculape by
Baccarat. Collection of The
John Nelson Bergstrom
Museum and Art Center,
Neenah, Wisconsin

Figs. XXIII & XXIV. Comte de Chambord by Baccarat (Left). Collection of The New-York Historical Society, New York, New York. Pope ? by Baccarat (Right). Collection of Corning Museum of Glass, Corning, New York

Fig. XXV. (Upper Left) Series of portraits by Boudon de Saint-Amans (?). (Upper Right) Duchesse d'Angoulême by Baccarat. (Bottom, Left to Right) General Blücher by Baccarat, Chateaubriand (?) by Baccarat, and Philibert Delorme by Baccarat. Author's Collection

Fig. XXVI. (Upper Left) Sadi-Carnot by Cristalleries de Clichy. (Upper Right) Queen Victoria and Prince Albert by Cristalleries de Clichy. (Bottom Left) Zachary Taylor by Cristalleries de Clichy. (Bottom Right) Louis-Philippe by Cristalleries de Clichy. Collection of The New-York Historical Society, New York, New York

Figs. XXVII & XXVIII. Saint Peter by Cristalleries de Clichy (Left). Collection of Corning Museum of Glass, Corning, New York. Queen Victoria and Prince Albert by Cristalleries de Clichy (Right). Collection of C. Frank Kirkerker, Jr., Plainfield, New Jersey

Fig. XXIX. (Left) John F. Kennedy and Mrs. Kennedy by Georges Simon and Cristal d'Albret. (Right) H.M. King Gustav of Sweden by Leo Holmgren and Cristal d'Albret. Author's Collection

Fig. XXX. Paperweights of unknown origin. Collection of The Art Institute of Chicago, Chicago, Illinois

Fig. XXXI. Satin glass bowl with applied cameo incrustations of Queen Victoria on front and back; 6″ diameter; signed "Webb" (Thomas Webb and Sons). Collection of Albert Christian Revi

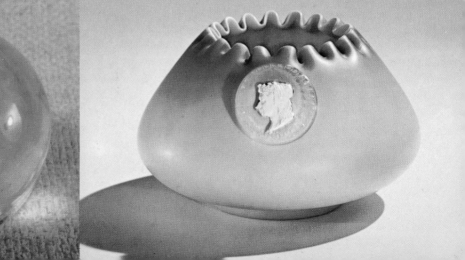

Fig. 89. Louis XVIII by Baccarat.
Collection of Musée des Arts
Décoratifs, Bordeaux, France

positions, such as *agate, alabaster,* and *rice paste,* which are
sold today by antique dealers as collector's items.

In 1838 an executive at Baccarat, Monsieur de Fontenay, dis-
covered the way of making colored lead crystal, a hitherto
closely guarded secret of the Bohemian glass industry. In 1846

Fig. 90. Sulphides of the Duc de Bordeaux by Baccarat. *Collection of Musée des Arts Décoratifs, Bordeaux, France*

Fig. 91. Sulphide of General Lafayette after the bronze bust, which was presented to President Monroe after the general was a guest of the nation in 1824 and 1825. The bust is now in the library of the James Monroe Memorial Foundation, Fredericksburg, Virginia. *Author's Collection*

Fig. 92. Paperweights (Top) General Lafayette by Baccarat (?). Collection of Edward S. Thompson, Maryville, Kentucky. (Bottom) Chateaubriand by Baccarat. Collection of Paul Loraine, Esquire, London, England

Fig. 93. William Pitt by Baccarat, from a ceramic by Leonard James Abington. Collection of Musée des Arts Décoratifs, Paris, France

91

the factory perfected a new type of article, the "cameo" and the "millefiori" (one thousand flowers) paperweights. The fine flower-like canes or the cameos portraying famous individuals, as well as lifelike fruits, butterflies, or snakes, were eventually incorporated into ornamental pieces and even tableware.

One of Baccarat's blowers, named Robinet, can also be credited with the invention in 1824 of the pump that bears his name and is still used today to facilitate the blowing of certain large, heavy ornamental pieces. In 1885 Baccarrat perfected hydrofluoric-acid etching and from 1840 to 1880 worked endlessly on devising and improving machines that could replace man on simple cutting jobs.

Baccarat's successful striving for perfection and prestige over two centuries was the result of a unity of purpose that would seem to reflect prosperity or economic stability. Yet it was achieved through revolutions and social upheavals, wars, foreign invasions, and economic crises. The French Revolution was followed by political upsets in 1830, 1848, and 1870. The Napoleonic Wars were followed by the invasion of eastern and northern France by foreign troops, a fact repeated for periods

Fig. 94. Baccarat plaques. (*Left to Right*) King Carl XIV Johan of Sweden and Norway, from a medal by Jean Jacques Barré; Queen Desirée of Sweden and Norway, wife of King Carl XIV, from a medal by Jean Jacques Barré; and Eugène Beauharnais, from a medal by Franz Xaver Lösch. *Collection of the Royal Palace, Stockholm, Sweden*

Fig. 95. (*Top, Left to Right*) J. François Regnard, from a medal by F. Dubois; P. Jolyot de Crébillon, from a medal by Depaulis; and Nicolas Poussin, from a medal by Dubois. (*Bottom, Left to Right*) Charles d'Alberg, Grand Duc de Francfort; Boileau, from a medal by Depaulis (?); and Marie Rabutin de Sévigné, from a medal by Gayrard. *Author's Collection, except for the sulphide of Charles d'Alberg, which is part of a Private Collection, Paris, France.* Below are the medals for the sulphides of Regnard, Crébillon, Poussin, and Mme. de Sévigné.

Fig. 96. An extremely rare sulphide paperweight of the Death Mask of Napoleon I resting on a cushion, from a medal by Depaulis. Napoleon's remains were returned from St. Helena on May 5, 1821. *Collection of Albert Christian Revi, Hanover, Pennsylvania*

ranging from a few weeks to four or five years in 1870, 1914, and 1940 when enemy troops occupied Baccarat. The factory suffered some shell damage but otherwise was ready to resume its activity at the end of World War II in 1945.

War on French soil and enemy occupation were not the only crises that Baccarat had to meet during its long history. Foreign wars, revolutions, or economic depressions disrupted markets and called for constant readjustments: the Civil War in the United States, the Austro-Prussian War in 1866, the Balkan Wars of 1896 and following years, the Spanish-American War of 1898, the Russian Revolution of 1917, which deprived Baccarat of its largest foreign market, and the Depression of 1929 that shook the world.

The corporation became the "Compagnie des Cristalleries de Vonêche-Baccarat" in 1824. On January 1, 1843, its charter was renewed for 40 years under the name of "Compagnie des Cristalleries et Verreries de Baccarat"; it was renewed a second time, in 1881 for 60 years, under the name, "Compagnie des Cristalleries de Baccarat," and finally for 99 years in 1941. The present Baccarat showroom, on the rue de Paradis, in Paris, with its 265-foot-long main room, its mezzanine, its sprawling galleries, and its museum, dates back to 1831 on the same spot.

The heart of the Baccarat factory today is really the center mall, a rectangular common about 250 yards long and 100 yards wide. It is bounded at one end by the chateau, residence of the managing director, and at the other end by the furnace hall; the sides are lined by the rows of workers' homes and the administration building. Some of the beautiful trees, part of the chateau's park, are centuries old. The mall is reminiscent of a small town square. Children play there after school, while a few mongrel dogs go lazily about. Hens peck in the chateau's garden. Workers' wives gossip from door to door. With its 1,000 workers, most of whom were born and raised on the premises, generation after generation, with its school for children and apprentices, with its chapel, the factory is truly the heart of the town of Baccarat; nearly every family there derives its livelihood directly or indirectly from it.

CRISTALLERIES
DE CLICHY

Very little is known about this factory, which is unfortunate, since Clichy produced some of the most beautiful paperweights, with sulphides on deep color grounds, although we have not identified any other objects with cameo incrustations from this company. Messrs. Rouyer and Mass founded a glass factory in 1738 at Sèvres, near Paris, transferred it in 1844 to Clichy, a Paris suburb, and were soon very successful in their enterprise. A few years later the Clichy factory manufactured a kind of glass without lead but which was found even clearer than the finest crystal. Their colored glass was of the highest quality. Around 1885 the factory was sold to a M. Landier, who had a factory in Sèvres. This sale was really the end of the outstanding production of the Cristalleries de Clichy.

CRISTALLERIES
DE SAINT LOUIS

The manufacture of glass in Lorraine was a trade of long standing. The discoveries of Gallic-Roman fragments in the Sarrebourg region and the establishment there of the first glassworks before the fifteenth century confirm this fact.

MUNSTHAL GLASS-WORKS (1586)

In 1469, by the Charter of the Glassmakers, the Duc de Lorraine decreed that free food, lodging, and transportation be given the workers of these glass houses. Because of these privileges, several glassworks were established in the district of Bitche (in the far eastern portion of the Moselle) during the fifteenth century. There, all the materials necessary for the production of glass could be found together: wood from extensive forests—the only fuel then in use—sand derived from the gritty earth, the salt marshes of Haute Sarre, and potash extracted from the ashes of ferns. In 1586, the Munsthal Glass-Works, direct ancestor of the Royal Glass-Works of St. Louis, was first mentioned. Its prosperity, alas, would be of short duration due to the wars of the seventeenth century and especially to the Thirty Years' War (1618-1648) which soon ruined the region.

THE ROYAL GLASS-WORKS OF ST. LOUIS (1767)

In 1766, Stanislas, Duc de Lorraine, died and Lorraine was united with France. At this time, René-François Jolly and Pierre-Étienne Ollivier, two lawyers at the supreme court of Lorraine and Barrois at Nancy, presented a request to the new sovereign; the answer was the decree of February 17, 1767, confirmed by the patent of March 4, 1767. Louis XV and his council of state, represented by the Duc de Choiseul "grant M. René-François Jolly & Company the perpetual tax free use of the Site at Munsthal for the building of a glass factory there." Also at their disposal were 8,000 acres, about 1,600 hectares, of wooded land from the Bitche forest to construct the buildings and to heat the kilns. Such an area was necessary to avoid deforestation, an unavoidable damage when the glass houses were itinerant.

This decree also gave this new glass house the title of "Royal Glass-Works of Saint Louis." Barely a year later, fine hollow glassware and table glassware made by this company were on the market. The year 1768 marked the arrival of two new partners, François de LaSalle, Sr., and Albert de LaSalle, joining with the founders. Then F. de LaSalle bought out the founders' shares and formed a new company, François de LaSalle, Sr., & Co.

THE MANUFACTURE OF LEAD CRYSTAL (1789)

But it was in 1789 that an outstanding event occurred: M. de Beaufort, director of the glass house, succeeded in reproducing lead crystal. Soon the hour of consecration would ring. It was the meeting of the Royal Academy of Science on January 12, 1782. These celebrities, among others, were present: Cassini, Lalande, Condorcet, Monge, Laplace, Lamarck, Daubenton, Lavoisier. . . . The academy examined the different pieces (water glasses, cups) presented by Messrs. de LaSalle and de Beaufort, respectively owner and director of the Royal Glass-Works of St. Louis. The comparison with English crystal pieces confirmed its perfect similarity in every way with the English product (clarity, specific weight, possible use for the lenses of achromatic glasses). The record of the meeting is signed "Condorcet." The new crystal of M. de Beaufort thus received the commendation of the Academy and warm encouragement: "It will advance our commerce and it might even become useful to Science." At the May 25, 1784, decree, the State Council recognized officially that "the manufacture of French crystal has reached the same degree of perfection as that of England." The decree further states: "There must be a resulting advantage for the commerce and for the state with a substantial lessening of spending outside of the country."

The result of this discovery was the great prosperity of St. Louis thus described by the Baron de Dietrich, a member of the Academy of Science: "There were 4 melting kilns, 3 of them constantly working; 12 kilns to spread out pane glass and table glass, 10 of these in use; 13 kilns or small arches to dry out the billets used in melting glass; 1 kiln to burn the fire-clays; a grindery, a potter's atelier and several other work-shops and store rooms. . . ." Life settled down around the factory; headquarters, offices, and buildings for the workers housed a total of 637 persons. There was also a church, a school, a doctor, and so forth.

In 1789, the Baron Maurice du Coetlosquet, Mestre de Camp and Dame Charlotte-Eugenie LaSalle, his wife, become sole owners of the St. Louis Glass-Works, valued at 300,000 pounds on their marriage settlement.

In 1785, a State Council's decree protected the glass house from the resignation of its employees. Workers were forbidden to leave without giving a 2-year notice, nor could they travel more than a mile without permission.

According to Dietrich, in 1788, St. Louis was one of the finest glassmaking establishments in the kingdom. These figures attest to this statement: "240,000 pounds in yearly sales, 76 workers for the manufacture of crystal, 61 workers for the manufacture of glass pane, out of a total of 360 to 400 persons."

Between 1791 and 1795, St. Louis was directed by Aime Gabriel d'Artigues. There he acquainted himself with the manufacture of crystal before buying back the Belgian Glass-works of Vonêche (Province of Namur) in 1802. This factory would become, in 1825, the Glassworks of Val St. Lambert, near Liège. In 1816, upon the closing of the French Trade, following the Treaty of Vienne, Mr. d'Artigues bought the St. Anne Glassworks at Baccarat for 862 hectograms of gold.

THE REVOLUTIONARY PERIOD (1798-1830)

The St. Louis Glass-Works, nationalized by the emigration of its owners, was offered for sale in 1798. The new owners, unwilling to manage it, leased it to Messrs. Seiler and Walter

Fig. 97. Napoleon I by Cristalleries de Saint Louis, from a medal by Denon commemorating the conquest of Egypt. *Collection of Cristalleries de Saint Louis Museum, Saint Louis, France*
Below are the two sides of the medal.

who, in turn, bought it in 1809. A twelfth of the shares was given back to the previous owners upon their return from emigration. In 1829, the firm of Seiler Walter & Co., then a Limited Company under the name of "Glass and Crystal Company of St. Louis," had assets of 1,200,000 francs in 120 shares. This was the beginning of a second era of great prosperity. Indeed, in 1820, St. Louis was the first company to press glass in a mould to obtain pressed crystal pieces, with sharp chamfers, an impossible achievement with the ordinary glass-blowing method.

THE ERA OF LAUNAY-HAUTIN (1830-1848)

In 1831, the two principal glass houses of eastern France became closer. Their directors, Messrs. Seiler and Godard, were in constant contact and joined forces to sell their products. They owned a joint sales warehouse in Paris, on the rue de Paradis, from 1831 to 1857. In 1832, the glassworks of St. Cloud, transferred to Mont-Cenis, near the Creusot, was acquired by Baccarat and St. Louis. They resold it in 1837 to the Schneider Company. St. Louis was therefore co-owner, for a while, of what was the "cradle" of the present Creusot. This is the most outstanding era for the manufacture of paperweights and sulphides that would later be worth very high prices.

During this period colored hollow glassware in one, two, or more layers and opalines began to be manufactured, the first in 1844, appearing in white, light blue, amber-yellow, rice paste, colored agates.

Generally speaking, this period was characterized by a considerable search for new shapes and colorings. The quality was also improved by the use of purer raw materials. This was also the golden age of glass manufacture under protection of tariff barriers. The shapes of glassware show an interesting evolution—the cone-shaped goblet and the waisted goblet of the eighteenth century gave way to the cylindrical goblet. The glass stem was bulky, sometimes with a knob, and ended with a round or square foot. In 1834, there was a "verre gondole" in eight different sizes and eight sizes in goblets.

This era was the true awakening of fine tableware, with carafes, fruit bowls, and many other pieces being manufactured.

FROM 1855 TO 1870

At the time of the Universal Exposition of 1855, the St. Louis Glass-Works was one of the top business industries in France, rated by its output and by the number of employees. It manufactured for home consumption and for exportation about 2 million francs' worth of white crystals, plain, pressed moulded, colored, cut, engraved, and decorated; it maintained over 1,500 employees, both skilled workers and laborers, not counting the 300 to 400 lumberjacks and carters used most of the year for the cutting and transportation of wood for fuel. It had a covered area containing 4 large melting kilns, 4 cutteries with 500 wheels activated by six 80-horsepower steam engines; it owned vast storerooms, ateliers for making red lead, crucibles, and potash. Numerous lodgings available for the executives, employees, and workers were scattered in different villages close to the factory.

After the departure of M. d'Artigues in 1795, Jacques Seiler took over the management (1797-1817), followed by François-Antoine Seiler (1817-1857). Then François-Antoine's nephew, Louis Lorin was director (1857-1858); next came Adolphe Marcus, son-in-law of Louis Lorin, who was replaced by Eugène Didierjean (1863-1895).

During the period of 1860-1895, the quality of the products

was improved by the more scientific handling of the raw materials. Wood was replaced by coal in the kilns. The last wood-burning kiln was put out in 1866; the first Siemens coal-gas kiln and regenerators were used in 1863. A few Boetius coal kilns operated between 1855 and 1864. The management, during this same period, abolished work on Sunday, established individual payment for work done, and outlined the idea of a common fund for sickness and retirement.

In 1860, following the signature of the French-English trade treaty lowering the custom duties, the company deliberately manufactured for export trade. In 1867, the business volume was valued at 3,400,000 gold francs (45 per cent being for exportation).

FROM 1870 TO 1913

The second half of the nineteenth century was marked by the disturbances of the Franco-Prussian War of 1870. During the German siege of Bitche, the three kilns were turned off on the eighth of August. One kiln was started again in September and the workers used it every other week, but it was not until the middle of 1871 that the other two kilns were lighted again. Difficulties were such that the situation did not improve until 1877. The company then developed its line of glass kerosene lamps and lighting fixtures for train compartments. It had a sample room in Berlin. In 1900, St. Louis employed over 2,000 persons.

After M. Eugène Didierjean's lengthy management, with the help of Messrs. Gustave Seiler and Maurice du Coetlosquet, came to an end, there was a period of instability. This was owing to the difficulty in finding a French director for this

French enterprise located in annexed Lorraine. Messrs. Georgel and Philipp ran the firm following the departure of Messrs. Jules Amiet, François Villain, and Consigny. Georgel was the general director until 1937; Philipp was the manager of the factory until 1939.

WORLD WAR I (1914-1919)

What was the position of St. Louis just previous to World War I? All markets were opened: Germany, Russia, North America, France. In fact, it was represented the world over and enjoyed a reputation without equal. Messrs. Georgel and Philipp witnessed, one from the French side, the other from the German side, the war of 1914-1918, which brought about the seizure of the Paris warehouse and factory.

In 1917, the German administration, short of fuel, closed down all nonessential industries, and the kilns stayed closed until February 1, 1919.

FROM 1920 TO 1939

Although the years 1920 to 1930 were euphoric ones and saw the growth of its trade-mark in numerous markets (United States, France, South America), the depression did touch the St. Louis Glass-Works because its domestic market was still poorly established. The manpower of the factory was thus cut down from 1,300 to 800.

During 1937, the company's contract, which had been renewed for fifty years in 1887, expired. The local Alsace-Lorraine legal company was changed into a Limited company governed by French rules.

WORLD WAR II (1939-1945)

In 1939, the factory was working with two kilns, one with eighteen pots, the other with twelve, under the general management of André de Guerre, son of the former president, Albert de Guerre (1904-1917). Sensing the coming conflict, M. de Guerre sent the maximum merchandise to Paris in 1939. The company employed at this time 804 workers, 200 of whom were glassblowers. The factory being located immediately behind the Maginot Line, the transformation of office and warehouse buildings into a hospital was foreseen and, indeed, was effected at the end of 1939. When war was declared, kilns were stopped and 200 workers from the factory were mobilized.

Next came the occupation and the integration into the German economy. The factory was confiscated. The village suffered from several bombings at the end of 1944 and at the beginning of 1945. (There were five civilian victims.) This difficult time lasted until March, 1945. On August 1, 1945, the factory reopened its doors, employing 120 cutters. Then one kiln with eighteen pots was lighted again on March 11, 1946; the one with 12 pots was relighted on December 1, 1946. The reorganization of such a complex unit posed multiple problems—human, material, and financial. André de Guerre (general manager until 1951) and Georges Clavel (general manager from 1952 to 1957) had also to face difficulties raised by economic measures, such as the freezing of prices, which were ill-adjusted to the manufacture of hand-production of luxury items. Georges Clavel, interrupted by death in his work of modernization, did not see better times. Today, however, crystal is worked in detail as it was for nearly two centuries by qualified and specialized hand production.

ST. LOUIS TODAY

Vicomte du Breil de Pontbriand and M. André Didierjean, (general manager) watch over St. Louis' destiny today. Its production places the company among the largest manufacturing establishments of the world. During these last years, the company has made important renovations and has updated and modernized its equipment with very modern cutting workshops, oil-heated kilns, and mixers for the crystal composition. But the Glass-Works has retained the same spirit and the skillful hand production associated with its village for centuries, and is jealous of its tradition.

JOHN FORD
AND COMPANY

We are most grateful to Mr. George A. Young, Superintendent of City Museums of Edinburgh, Scotland, who has given us the following information about the John Ford Company and the pictures of sulphides now in the Huntly House Museum.

In 1812, a William Ford, whose family probably originally came from Newcastle, had established himself in the North Back of the Canongate, in what was known as the Caledonian Glass Works. Three years later he had moved over to the South Back of the Canongate and established a glassworks there which was to become the best known of all the Edinburgh glass houses and to be owned and controlled by the Ford family for nearly a hundred years.

After the death of William Ford, a company was formed to run the business and among the directors in this company was his nephew, John Ford. This company was dissolved in 1835, and the business was thereafter personally conducted by John

Fig. 98. These two plaques showing a glassblower and a glass-engraver still adorn the front of the building originally used by John Ford and Co., but now occupied by a brewery and part of a tenement.

Ford. In the *Edinburgh Gazette* for Friday, July 31, 1835, John Ford announced that "he will conduct business in future at the glass works, South Back of Canongate, in the premises formerly occupied by the company, now the 'Holyrood Flint Glass Works.' " One of the first glasses made after John Ford took over is in the Ford Ranken collection in Huntly House, Edinburgh, and has engraved on it: "Manufactured at the Holyrood Flint Glass Works, Canongate, Edinburgh, on the first day of their commencement, the 10th August, 1835."

Under John Ford's ownership the works began to expand rapidly and the variety of goods to increase. By the middle of the century the Holyrood Glass Works were by far the most extensive in the area and selling their goods, not only in the home market but as far away as Copenhagen, Berlin, Hamburg, and other continental cities.

Fig. 99. Duke of Wellington by John Ford and Co.; diamond-engraved on one side "Wellington," and on the other side "Holyrood Glass Works." (Twice actual size) *Collection of Royal Scottish Museum, Edinburgh, Scotland*

In 1837, John Ford was appointed Flint Glass Manufacturer in ordinary to Queen Victoria. Possibly in celebration of this appointment, a huge epergne, thirty-nine inches high, was cut. The finial is in the shape of a Maltese Cross, resembling the cross on the imperial crown. This very fine specimen of deep crystal cutting was carried out by Richard Hunter, the foreman cutter, and took two years to complete, being finished in 1840. The epergne was exhibited at the Edinburgh Exhibition in 1886, and it was placed by command on the Royal Table at the State dinner at Holyrood Palace on the occasion of H.M. King George V's first official visit to Edinburgh on August 25, 1911. It was presented to the City in 1960 by Mrs. Ford Ranken and family and can be seen at the City Museum, Huntly House.

The appointment of Flint Glass Manufacturer to the Queen was no mere formality. Queen Victoria was a regular customer, having standing orders for small mugs, given to her many god children at their christening, and goblets, engraved with Balmoral Castle, as wedding gifts. In 1898 permission was granted to change the firm's name to the Royal Holyrood Glass Works.

Under John Ford's enterprising management every description of table ornament, crystal and glass, was manufactured and cut. All shades of color were tried and new designs were continually being added. From their recipe books of the period it can be seen that they were constantly trying some new mixture of ingredients to improve and vary their wares. They were obtaining their sands from places as far away as Lynn, Norfolk, and the Isle of Wight. The lead came from Birmingham or Liverpool, although it appears that the latter was not very satisfactory. The variety and number of articles produced at this time was quite astonishing. In a traveller's book dated

Fig. 100. (Left) Robert Burns by John Ford and Co.; signed "Moore." *(Right)* George Heriot by John Ford and Co.; signed "Wood." *Collection of Royal Scottish Museum, Edinburgh, Scotland*

1842 there are listed for sale sugar bowls, chemical bottles, cruets, confection jars, custard cups, all kinds of wine glasses, decanters, root glasses, goblets, and tumblers. An entry for September, 1856, shows the surprising extent of their sales market listing nineteen merchants in Glasgow alone to whom they sold goods. The English journey took the traveller to such places as Liverpool, York, Leeds, Sheffield, Chesterfield, and Derby.

One of their most successful "gimmicks" begun about this time was the introduction of a coin in the specially prepared space in the stem of their goblets and in the base of tumblers. This idea was so successful that goblets and tumblers with coins were produced right up to 1904. The most popular years were, of course, 1887 and 1897, the jubilee years of Queen Victoria's reign. Another successful innovation was the inclusion of cameos into paperweights and bottles of different kinds. These cameos were usually of such famous people as Shake-

Fig. 102. (Left) William Ewart Gladstone by John Ford and Co.; signed "L.C. Wyon F." *(Right)* Queen Anne by John Ford and Co. *Collection of Royal Scottish Museum, Edinburgh, Scotland*

speare, Byron, Scott, and Wellington. These were not original ideas, however, as some glass works in the south had already tried them out successfully.

The Holyrood Glass Works expanded rapidly and by the middle of the century over two hundred men were employed in the factory. It is reported in a local newspaper of 1886 that the glass workers in the Ford factory were getting steady work and occasionally overtime, so that they were able to make "fabulous" wages, at least more than £2 per week!

In the early eighteen sixties a very talented glass engraver, Millar (or Müller), a Bohemian, established himself in the neighborhood. A very close cooperation began between the Holyrood Glass Works and Millar and his son, J. H. B. Millar, which was to continue for many years. Millar's work began to appear on many of the major pieces of Holyrood glass and so much of his work was for the Holyrood Glass Works that

Fig. 101. Prince Albert by John Ford and Co. (Twice actual size) *Collection of Royal Scottish Museum, Edinburgh, Scotland*

117

Fig. 103. Vase with cameo of Gladstone by John Ford and Co.; signed "L.C. Wyon." *Author's Collection*

his business was almost an adjunct of the Holyrood Glass Works. The engraving of J. H. B. Millar was of the highest quality, no matter what the subject. Flowers, trees, birds, and animals were his favorites, although he was particularly fond of classical designs with Greek and Roman figures. It was about this time that the famous fern design, so distinctive of Holyrood Glass, began to appear and continued to do so right up to the closure of the glass works.

In May, 1865, John Ford died and the firm became John Ford & Company, being carried on most successfully by the partnership of his son, William Ford, and Francis Ranken. The Rankens were a well-known Edinburgh family in the same line of business, and in the next generation William Ranken married Pauline, daughter of William Ford, thus uniting two families of glassmakers. Under this partnership the firm enjoyed one of its most successful periods. Their goods

Fig. 104. Caroline Bonaparte by John Ford and Co.; signed "Andrieu." (Actual height: 12 inches) *Author's Collection*

Fig. 105. Paperweight from an unknown English factory. *Author's Collection*

were being bought all over the country and, breaking into a new export market, they had great success at the Sydney International Exhibition of 1897 and at the Melbourne Exhibition the following year. Nearly five hundred different articles are listed as being sent to the Sydney Exhibition and three hundred and fifty sets of glasses to Melbourne. The engraving for the latter showed an Australian influence, the kangaroo, for instance, replacing the Scottish deer. The large amount of articles available for these exhibitions illustrates the scope of their manufacture of goods at this time and many pieces originally designed for these exhibitions were being produced continually up to the time when the factory closed.

The Holyrood Glass Works had a prominent stand at the Edinburgh Exhibition of 1886 at which they also gave practical demonstrations of glass blowing and engraving, also sandblasting of designs onto cheaper domestic items, such as oil and lamp-glasses. Unfortunately the latter articles are rarely seen nowadays.

An additional venture at this time was the acquisition of a shop of their own in fashionable Princes Street, and also a branch warehouse in Union Street, Aberdeen.

In 1896 the factory had the honor of making the wedding gift from the City of Edinburgh to the Duke and Duchess of York, who later became King George V and Queen Mary. This consisted of 256 delicate pieces of tableware beautifully engraved with coats of arms and national emblems. Specimens of these are in the Holyrood Glass collection at Huntly House Museum.

Toward the end of the nineteenth century the factory began to import some glass, especially Bohemian, and engrave their own designs on it. This was unfortunate from many points of view and is now confusing the historian and collector.

In 1904 the factory closed down. Part of the site is now occupied by a tenement on the front of which are two panels depicting a glass blower and a glass cutter, which used to decorate the front wall of the Royal Holyrood Glass Works. (Fig 98). The retail business of John Ford was carried on by William Ranken until 1924, when his son succeeded him in the business. He died in 1959 when, though the good will of the firm was taken over by the purchaser, the name of Ford expired.

MODERN SULPHIDES

The art of making sulphides was revived in 1952 when we asked the Cristalleries de Baccarat and the Cristalleries de Saint Louis to produce cameo paperweights as they did in the 1840's.

Baccarat's first subject was General Dwight D. Eisenhower, followed by a paperweight for the coronation of H.M. Queen Elizabeth II of England and H.R.H. the Duke of Edinburgh.

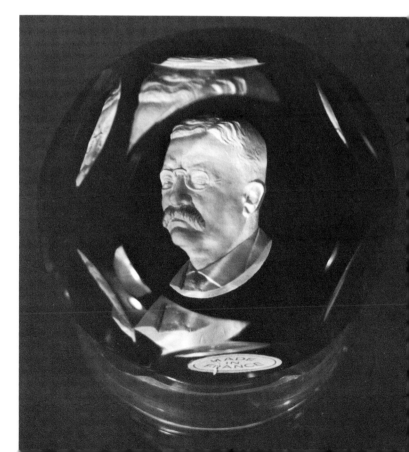

Fig. 106. Theodore Roosevelt by Baccarat. *Author's Collection*

Fig. 107. Saint Louis, King of France, by
J. H. Coëffin, after sculpture by unknown
artist. *Author's Collection*

Fig. 108. View of the Cristalleries et Verreries de Vianne. (Cristal d'Albret).

Since then Baccarat has produced cameo incrustations of the following subjects: Lincoln, Washington, Churchill, Jefferson, Queen Elizabeth II, Robert E. Lee, Franklin, Lafayette, Luther, Pope Pius XII, Sam Rayburn, John F. Kennedy, Pope John XXIII, Theodore Roosevelt, Will Rogers. These cameos were sculptured by three great French artists: Gilbert Poillerat, Dora Maar, and Albert David.

The Cristalleries de Saint Louis produced a sulphide of H.M. Queen Elizabeth II in 1952. However they discontinued their production until June, 1967, when a cameo was designed of Saint Louis, King of France, by Mrs. J. Coëffin, of the French Mint, to commemorate the bi-centennial of the Cristalleries de Saint Louis.

125

Another company, formed less than fifty years ago, the Cristalleries et Verreries de Vianne (Cristal d'Albret), is now making sulphide paperweights. Three were produced in 1967: Christopher Columbus, Franklin D. Roosevelt, and John F. Kennedy and Mrs. Kennedy in the same sulphide. These cameos were sculptured by the well-known artist, Georges Simon, of the French Mint. (Fig. XXIX.)

This art of cameo incrustation lost for almost a century is alive again.

CRISTALLERIES ET VERRERIES DE VIANNE

In the heart of Gascogne, the part of France where Alexandre Dumas placed the cradle of his hero d'Artagan, and where Edmond Rostand made Cyrano de Bergerac live, there is, hidden behind its walls, ramparts and watchtowers, a very small town, very quiet and peaceful today. It was not always so peaceful and, indeed, very few places so small can boast of a past so full of struggle and fight, so bloody and tearful. Archaeology has proved that there was a human settlement there in the Stone Age; in 52 B.C. the Gascons were given the pompous title "Friends of the Romans"; one finds there ruins of the mint of the Merovingians, of tombs of the Carolingians; even these days, from time to time, one finds buried cases full of money that the Gascons sank into the earth during the numerous invasions. One that yielded the most valuable finds was from the first invasion of the Barbars in the year 276.

This small town was then called Villelongue. However, its master did not like that name and replaced it by the name of the "lady of his dreams." Since then the town goes by the name of Vianne. But in spite of this pretty name, the town continued to be torn to pieces by the English and the French, by Catholics and Protestants. During these religious wars, Cardinal de Richelieu bought a "baronny" in Vianne where he relaxed and recuperated from the duties imposed upon him by the Kingdom that was entirely at his mercy. The property was kept in his family until the Revolution.

Thanks to the protection of its walls, Vianne survived all those tribulations, all those wars, massacres, and devastations, without, however, being able to achieve any kind of durable prosperity. When finally the reign of Louis XVI arrived, and with it the abolition of freedoms and autonomies of the "Communes," the provinces were forced to adopt their policy to that of the Nation and to cease to be concerned only with their local affairs. Only then the region was pacified; only then the industries could take root, develop, and grow, and bring prosperity to Gascogne. In Vianne itself it was the glass industry that took root nearly half a century ago.

The present successor of the old tradition of glass manufacturing are the Cristalleries et Verreries de Vianne, which were reorganized in 1918 at the end of World War I.

These glassworks employ over 800 specialists and workmen and export their products all over the world. Since 1967 they have been producing sulphide paperweights.

BIOGRAPHY OF
MEDALLISTS
AND SCULPTORS

Andrieu, Bertrand, 1761-1822, French. Born in Bordeaux. At age 8 became a pupil of André Lavan, an engraver of armorial bearings. In 1786 he went to Paris and entered the die makers business. Andrieu was at the head of the School of Engravers which flourished under the First French Empire. His style combines the "noble elegance of the Greeks with the charming truths of nature so much admired in Warin and Dupré." In 1800, the first consul, Bonaparte, having made his friend Devon Directeur Général of the Museums, a series of medals was begun, destined to celebrate his eventful rule. In this work, Andrieu's collaboration was secured. In 1812, his reputation made, he was elected a member of the Imperial Academy of Vienna and several princes ordered medals from him: Prince Emil Leopold Augustus, Duke of Saxe-Gotha-Altenburg, Queen Hortense,

129

Princesses Pauline, and Eliza Bonaparte. His idealized head of Napoleon served for the obverse of the greater number of the Napoleonic series of medals; others were Birth of Duke of Bordeaux and his baptism. He died December 10, 1822.

He engraved a steel plate for a 1000-franc note of 1817. One of the best engravers of his time, he was unsurpassed by any of his contemporaries, execpt perhaps Droz. He often engraved the dies direct—showing his sureness of hand and wonderful skill.

Paris Mint Museum possesses 79 medals and *jetons* by Andrieu.

BARRÉ, JEAN JACQUES, 1795-1855, French. Medallist and "Graveur Général des Médailles" from 1842 to 1855. Apprenticed to Thiolier at 17. First exhibit at the Salon of 1819. Works of his—medals, portraits, dies, etc.—at each year's Fine Art Exhibit. Cut Royal coins of Louis Philippe and official Seals of the National Assembly and State under the Second Republic. Napoleon on his election as President chose J. J. Barré's patterns for the new coinage, and the same portrait was used on the currency of the Third Empire. Engraved the plates for the Bank of France and those of the Banks of Rouen, Lyon, and Toulouse. Of his two sons, the eldest Jean Auguste was a sculptor of merit while the younger Désiré Albert succeeded his father in 1855 as Chief Engraver at the Paris Mint.

CAUNOIS, FRANCOIS AUGUSTIN, 1787-1859, French. Medallist, pupil of Dejoux. Made a large number of portrait-medals. His medal on the Coronation of Charles X (1825) is very beautiful. In 1813 he had obtained the second prize at the "Concours pour Rome." In 1815 he was awarded the position of *logiste* for medal engraving. In 1848 he submitted to the Coinage

Commission of the Second French Republic patterns for the gold, silver, and copper currency.

DEPAULIS, ALEXIS JOSEPH, 1792-1867, French. Medallist, pupil of Andrieu and Cartellier. 1813, Ecole des Beaux Arts; 1827, second class medals; 1833, first class medals; decorated with the Legion of Honor in 1834. Many portrait medals as well as others commemorating events: medals to commemorate the birth of the Duke of Bordeaux, the crowning of Charles X, the transfer of Napoleon's remains in 1840. Among them there is a marble medallion of Louis Philippe in the Chartres Museum.

DEVON, DOMINIQUE VIVANT, 1747-1825, French. Medallist, engraver, draughtsman, archaeologist, and writer. He was a member of the Institut de France, associate of the Academy of Dijon, Officer of the Legion of Honor, Knight of the Orders of St. Ann of Russia and of the Crown of Bavaria, and held in succession the post of diplomatist, artist, and public administrator. Was director of the Museums and of the Mint, an office he filled until 1815. Under Louis XVI, he occupied the place of the Keeper of the Medal Cabinet. Napoleon raised him to the rank of baron. Nearly all the medals, forming the medallic history of Napoleon I, which were struck at the Paris Medal Mint, and engraved by the artists Andrieu, Brenet, Droz, Dupré, Duvivier, Gatteaux, etc., bear Devon's signature. One of the pavilions of the Louvre bears his name.

DROZ, JEAN PIERRE, 1746-1823, Swiss. Celebrated coin-engraver and medallist. His father, a manufacturer of agricultural equipment taught him to work on metal, and at age 18 he was sent to Paris to learn engraving. In 1786 he made a beautiful pattern for an Ecu of Six Livres, struck both sides at the same time in one blow of the hammer and the edge bearing an inscription, in raised letters. He invented another new press. Later he introduced new processes but political events in the French government prevented him from getting the support he needed and he went to Birmingham, England, where he engraved English and foreign coins. When he returned to France in 1799 he was elected Keeper of the Coins and Medals. England showed their appreciation of him by saying that with all the improvements he had made in the art of coining, it was almost impossible to counterfeit coins. Orders came in from the governments all over the world to have him improve their mints. He was General Administrator of The Coins and Medals of France and Napoleon made him Keeper of the Coins and Medals of France. In 1815 he issued a pattern for a five-france piece of Napoleon I.

DUBOIS, JOSEPH EUGENE, 1795-1863, French. Born in Paris, died at Lignières-la-Doucelle (Mayenne). Pupil of Droz, he worked at the French Mint during the Restoration and made some beautiful medals: Parmentier, Hippocrates, Duchess of Berry, Duke of Bordeaux, King Joseph Bonaparte.

DUPRÉ, AUGUSTIN, 1748-1833, French. Goldsmith, medallist, and coin-engraver. General of the Coins under the First French Republic. He started quite early learning the manufacture of arms, and the study of chasing and sculpture. 1791-1803 office of Engraver General of the French coins. He did many kinds of work, with jewels, articles of plate, ornaments, and so forth, but his chief claim to fame is as a medallist and coin-engraver. He was a personal friend of Benjamin Franklin, of whom he made a medal. Worked with Duvivier.

DUVIVIER, PIERRE SIMON BENJAMIN, 1730-1819, French. Born and died in Paris. He was a member of the Painting Academy in 1776 and was received at the "Institut" in 1806. He produced some outstanding medals, Louis XV, Louis XVI, Prince of Condé, Cardinal de la Roche, among them.

GATTEAUX, JACQUES EDOUARD, 1788-1881, French. Sculptor and medallist. In 1809 he obtained the Prix de Rome. Pupil of the French Academy at Rome; when he returned to Paris he was called to the Office of the Medallist to Louis XVIII and executed a number of fine medals on the Peace of 1814, the Holy Alliance, and portrait-medallions of contemporaneous celebrities. Knighted in 1833; elected a member of the "Institut" in 1845. In 1861, made an Officer of the Legion of Honor. Between 1807-1847, 289 medals executed.

GAYRARD, RAYMOND, 1777-1858, French. Sculptor, medallist, and gem-engraver. Showed early talent, learned chasing and engraving, worked for goldsmiths. Devon helped him and he had a long series of successes. Knighted in 1825. Also a poet and moralist. Probably 300 medallions.

JALEY, LOUIS, 1763-1838, French. Medallist, pupil of Moitte and Dupré. Engraver of medals of the Napoleonic series.

MASSON, AUGUSTE, 1842-1870, French. Sculptor and medallist. All bronze medallions cast.

MOORE, JOSEPH, 1817-1901. Born in Birmingham. British. Medallist. Starting business for himself, he began with dies for button making which, at that time, was one of the chief industries of the town. He was awarded a prize for his work at the

1851 Exhibition. He worked at the Birmingham Mint making dies for currency. He designed a medal commemorating the visit of Queen Victoria to Birmingham in 1858. Among his finest medals we find those of the Duke of Wellington, Sir Charles Napier, Nathan Mayer Rothschild, Prince Oscar of Sweden, Robert Burns, Martin Luther.

PETIT, LOUIS MICHEL, 1791-1844, French. Sculptor and medallist. Many medals usually signed "L. M. Petit. F." or "Petit. F." Portrait medallist of the kings and queens of France. Member of the Committee of the Mint.

POSCH, LEONHARD, 1750-1831, German. Sculptor and medallist. Apprenticed to sculptor at Salzburg and settled in Vienna. For health reasons, he had to give up sculpture for modelling. Moved to Paris in 1810. Worked under Devon. Modelled portraits of princes and celebrated persons. Returned to Berlin in 1814. Obtained from the Prussian Royal Academy the privileges of an Academician. He was very successful in portraiture and a prolific worker.

WYON, LEONARD CHARLES, 1826-1891. British. Medallist, coin-engraver. Eldest son of William Wyon, born in one of the residences connected with the Royal Mint in London, England. He inherited his father's great skill in die engraving. At the age of 16 he made various medals as studies, some of which are preserved in the British Museum in London. He became Second Engraver at the Royal Mint in 1851 when he was only seventeen and succeded his father as Chief Engraver although the office became extinct on the decease of William Wyon.

BIOGRAPHY OF PORTRAIT SUBJECTS

ALBERT, PRINCE (Francis Charles Augustus Emmanuel), 1819-1861: Consort of Queen Victoria. He was the son of Ernest I, duke of Saxe-Coburg-Gotha.

ALEXANDER I, 1777-1825?: Czar of Russia.

ANGOULÊME, DUCHESSE D' (Marie Thérèse Charlotte), 1778-1851: As daughter of Louis XVI and later wife of Louis Antoine d'Angoulême, the duchesse was imprisoned by the revolutionists from 1792-1795. An ambitious woman, she was able to exert a large amount of political influence during the reigns of Louis XVIII and Charles X. She died in exile, however, at Frohsdorf, Austria.

ANNE, 1665-1714: Queen of England.

AUMALE, DUC D' (Henri Eugène Philippe Louis d'Orléans), 1822-1897: Son of Louis Philippe and of Marie Amelie. He joined the army when he was 17 years old and fought brilliantly in Algeria in 1843. He became Governor of the Africa French possessions when the Revolution of 1848 broke out. General Cavaignac took over his functions and the Duc d'Aumale went to England where he studied history. When he tried to publish in Paris his *History of the Princes de Condé* the police confiscated the books and it was only in 1869, at the end of the Empire that the first two volumes could be published. This same year the Duc d'Aumale lost his wife, Princess Caroline whom he married in 1844 and who gave him two sons, the Prince de Condé who died in Australia in 1866 and the Duc de Guise, who died in 1872. Having an enormous fortune, the Duc d'Aumale willed to the Institut in 1886 his Chantilly castle. In 1889 the Duc d'Aumale was allowed to return to France from Belgium where he had taken refuge after General Boulanger had expelled him from the army in 1886. He became a member of the Academy of Moral Sciences and wrote several historical and political volumes.

135

BEAUHARNAIS, EUGÈNE DE, 1781-1824: Son of Alexandre and Joséphine de Beauharnais. French general who served bravely in the campaigns of his stepfather, Napoleon I. He was made viceroy of Italy in 1805. After Napoleon's defeat, Beauharnais, who had married a Bavarian princess, lived in Munich under the titles of Duke of Leuchtenberg and Prince of Eichstätt.

BERRY, DUC DE (Charles Ferdinand), 1778-1820: The younger son of Charles X, he served in Condé's army against the French Revolution. When he was assassinated in 1820, the ultraroyalists used the incident to turn Louis XVIII even more strongly against the liberals.

BERRY, DUCHESSE DE (Caroline Ferdinande Louise), 1798-1870: Wife of the Duc de Berry and daughter of Francis I of Naples, she was exiled from France in 1830. She returned two years later to try and win the throne for Berry's posthumous son, who later became known as Henri, Comte de Chambord, but her attempts led to her imprisonment. However, the discovery that she had married an Italian alienated French sympathy to such an extent that Louis Philippe considered the situation safe and released her.

BOILEAU-DESPRÉAUX, NICOLAS, 1636-1711: This French poet and literary critic numbered among his friends Racine, Molière, and La Fontaine from whom he drew ideas which he expanded until he became known as the spokesman of classicism. His works include "L'Art Poétique" (1674), "Satires" (1716), "Épîtres" (1701). Revered in the eighteenth century as a "literary lawgiver," Boileau was later detested by the romantics.

BONAPARTE, CAROLINA, 1782-1839: As sister of Napoleon I, Carolina went to France in 1793 with the Bonaparte family and seven years later married General Murat. In 1814 she became Queen of Naples. When Napoleon had a son, her hopes of succession for her own child were destroyed, so she and Murat joined intrigues with enemies of Napoleon but were unsuccessful. Following the fall of Napoleon, Metternich, who was in love with Carolina, attempted to save Murat's throne, but the latter's rashness led to his execution and his wife was forced to flee to Austria.

BORROMEO, SAINT CARLO (1538-1584): One of the great figures of the Counter-Reformation. At the early age of 23, he was made a Cardinal, and soon after Archbishop of Milan. He was the first to establish seminaries, according to the decrees of the Council of Trent, which have served as the pattern for the education of the Catholic clergy even to the present time. He established the Confraternity of Christian Doctrine. Under his personal supervision it developed into a mighty organization, which has had worldwide influence through the centuries.

BURNS, ROBERT, 1759-1796: Scottish poet.

BYRON, GEORGE GORDON NOEL, 6th Baron Byron, 1788-1824: English poet whose work includes "Fugitive Pieces" (1806); "Childe Harold" (1812); "The Corsair" (1814); "Lara" (1814); "Prisoner of Chillon" (1816), and "Don Juan," an unfinished epic satire.

CARNOT, MARIE FRANÇOIS SADI, 1837-1894: President of the French Republic. He succeeded Jules Grévy, who resigned in 1887 as President of the Republic. On June 24, 1894 while he was visiting the Lyon exhibition an Italian anarchist, Santo Caserio, stabbed him to death.

CHAMBORD, COMTE DE (HENRI CHARLES FERDINAND MARIE DIEUDONNÉ D'ARTOIS), 1820-1883: The posthumous son of Charles Ferdinand, Duc de Berry, the Comte de Chambord's original title was Duc de Bordeaux. His grandfather, Charles X, abdicated in his favor in 1839 but he was never able to hold the throne, though the legitimists did recognize him as Henry V. He spent most of his life at Frohsdorf, Austria, after accompanying Charles X into exile.

CHARLES X, 1757-1836: This brother of Louis XVI and Louis XVIII, whom he succeeded, reigned as King of France from 1824-1830, leaving for England where he led the 'emigrés' when the Revolution broke out in July of 1789. He remained in that country until the restoration of the Bourbons in 1814. During the reign of Louis XVIII he was the leader of the ultraroyalist opposition which was able to succeed following the assassination of Charles X's son, the Duc de Berry. In 1829 an uncompromising reactionary, Jules Armand de Polignac, was appointed by Charles X as chief minister. In order to divert attention from France's internal troubles this man instigated the Algerian venture, an action which led to the July Revolution. When Charles X abdicated, it was in favor of his grandson, the Comte de Chambord, but the Duc d'Orléans, appointed lieutenant general of France by Charles X, was the one chosen to reign as Louis Philippe. Charles X passed the remainder of his life in England and Scotland.

CHASSÉ, BARON D. H., 1765-1849: Dutch general who served in the French army with distinction in 1787 but returned to his country after Napoleon's first abdication and was made Lieutenant General by William I.

CHATEAUBRIAND, VICOMTE FRANÇOIS RENÉ DE, 1768-1848: This writer was the founder of romanticism in France. After his return to France following a visit to the United States in 1791 he became an émigré in England where he remained until 1800. His first book was published in England: *Essai historique, politique et moral sur les révolutions*. He became the most important of the contemporary French authors following the publication of *Atala* in 1801 and *René* in 1802. Among his works we find *Les Aventures du dernier des Abencérage* and *Mémoires d'Outre-tombe*.

CHÉNIER, MARIE JOSEPH DE, 1764-1811: Brother of the French poet André de Chénier. He was a member of the Convention, then of the Tribunate. He wrote the *Épître sur la Calomnie* in which he defends himself against the accusation of having betrayed his brother, whom he vainly tried to free from prison and who died on the scaffold.

CRÉBILLON, pen name of PROSPER JOLYOT, 1674-1762: Some of the best-known works of this French dramatist include *Idoménée* (1705), *Électre* (1708), *Rhadamiste et Zénobie* (1711), *Catalina* (1748). His attempts to rival Voltaire earned him that author's vicious attacks which served to immortalize Crébillon. In 1731 he was elected to the French Academy. His son, Claude Prosper Jolyot de Crébillon, also became an author.

DALBERG, KARL THEODOR ANTON MARIA VON, 1744-1827: He was the last elector of Mainz, German archchancelor after the dissolution of the Empire. He was a protege of Napoleon who made him "grand duc de Francfort, President of the 'Diete' and Prince of the Rhine Confederation.

DELILLE, ABBE JACQUES, 1738-1813: French poet whose translation in verse of the *Georgiques* by Virgil brought him a prodigious reputation. He published a number of poems: "Les Jardins," "l'Imagination," "l'Homme des Champs," and translations of the *Aeneid* and of *Paradise Lost*. He can be considered as the precursor of the Romantics: Lamartine, Vigny, Victor Hugo were inspired by him although they pretended not to like his work.

DELORME, PHILIBERT, 1515-1570: One of the greatest of the French renaissance architects, Delorme served under both Francis I and Henri II. He completed the ballroom at Fontainebleau and designed the tomb of Francis I, but perhaps his finest work was the beautiful Château d'Anêt for Diane de Poitiers, mistress of Henri II, of which only a few fragments remain. In 1563 he was requested by Catherine de Médicis to design the Palais des Tuileries and this project occupied the remainder of his life.

FOY, MAXIMILIEN SÉBASTIEN, GENERAL, 1775-1825: After fighting in the Napoleonic Wars, Foy was elected Deputy in 1819. An orator as well as general, he enjoyed great popularity due to his defense of public liberties.

GEORGE III (George William Frederick), 1738-1820: This King of Great Britain and Ireland was the son of Frederick Louis, Prince of Wales, and grandson of George II whom he succeeded.

GEORGE IV (George Augustus Frederick), 1762-1830: The son of George III, as King of Great Britain and Ireland he married a Roman Catholic, Maria Anne Fitzherbert, in 1785, but this marriage was denied and in 1795 he was married again, for political reasons, to Princess Caroline of Brunswick. George IV took little part in the affairs of his country and his extravagance and dissolute habits made him hated by his subjects.

GLADSTONE, WILLIAM EWART, 1809-1898: British statesman. He served as Prime Minister four times (1868-74, 1880-85, 1886, and 1892-94).

GOETHE, JOHANN WOLFGANG VON, 1749-1832: German poet, dramatist, and scientist, best known for *Faust*.

GUSTAVUS VI (Gustaf Adolf), 1882-: King of Sweden since 1950.

HENRY IV, 1553-1610: This King of France and of Navarre, son of Antoine de Bourbon and Jeanne d'Albret, was the first of the Bourbon kings of France.

HERIOT, GEORGE, 1563-1624: Famous Edinburgh goldsmith, who was jeweler to James VI of Scotland (James I of England).

JOAN OF ARC (Jeanne d'Arc), 1412-1431: At the age of 16, she led the armies of the Dauphin, Charles XII, against the English, who were trying to keep him from the throne. She was tried for heresy and sorcery, convicted and burned at the stake. In 1909 she was beatified and in 1920 canonized.

JOINVILLE, PRINCE DE, (François Ferdinand Philippe Louis Marie d'-Orléans), 1818-1900: Third son of King Louis Philippe. He joined the Naval Academy in 1834 and became a captain after the capture of the fort of Saint-Jean d'Ulloa (1839) and for his great courage at Veracruz. He brought back the ashes of Napoleon to France in 1840 and went into exile in 1848. He returned to France in 1871 when he was elected to the National Assembly and was given back his commission of Vice Admiral.

LAMBALLE, PRINCESSE DE, (Marie Thérèse Louise de Savoie-Carignan), 1749-1792: A favorite of Marie Antoinette, the princess was very unpopular with the people. During the September massacres she was killed by a mob, after which her head was placed under the queen's windows, displayed on a pike.

LAFAYETTE, MARQUIS DE (Marie Joseph Paul Yves Roch Gilbert du Motier), 1757-1834: French military leader and statesman. Because of his sympathy for the American cause in the Revolutionary War, Lafayette offered his services to Congress, which gave him in 1777 a commission as major general in the Continental Army. He became very close to George Washington and was a member of his staff.

LOUIS XVI, 1754-1793: King of France; married to Marie Antoinette.

LOUIS XVII (Louis Charles), 1785-1795, second son of Louis XVI and Marie Antoinette. He was imprisoned in 1792 with the royal family, and, after the execution of Louis XVI (1793) he was proclaimed king as Louis XVII but he died in prison in 1795.

LOUIS XVIII, 1755-1824: The brother of Louis XVI and Charles X, as King of France he was forced to flee in 1791 from the French Revolution to Coblenz but was recognized by the émigrés as regent following the death of Louis XVII in 1795. Napoleon hunted him through Europe but he was made king in 1814 after the allies entered Paris. He had to flee again when Napoleon returned and then came back with the allies after Waterloo. His influence was reduced after the second restoration and civil liberties were curbed.

LOUIS PHILIPPE, 1773-1850: Before his accession to the throne of France he was a member of the forces of the French Revolution (known then as Louis Philippe, Duc d'Orléans) but deserted in 1793 from the French Army. He spent a long while in exile in England and the United States. Following the Bourbon restoration he returned to France where he became a prominent figure of the opposition to Louis XVIII and Charles X.

MARIE LOUISE, 1791-1847: Marie Louise was Empress of the French and Duchess of Parma, Piacenza, and Guastella. She was the wife of Napoleon I and mother of Napoleon II.

MONTESPAN, MARQUISE DE (Françoise Athénais Rochechouart), 1641-1707: Mistress of Louis XIV.

MOZART, WOLFGANG AMADEUS, 1756-1791: Born in Salzburg, Austria. Mozart composed in all forms—church music, arias, songs, serenades, chamber music, sonatas, concertos, symphonies, operas—but his main interest seems to have been opera.

MURAT, JOACHIM, 1767-1815: Marshal of France and king of Naples, Murat fought under Napoleon in Egypt. In 1800 he married Napoleon's sister, Carolina Bonaparte, and in 1808 he succeeded Joseph Bonaparte to the throne of Naples.

NAPOLEON I (Napoleon Bonaparte), 1769-1821: Emperor of France.

NAPOLEON II, 1811-1832: Known as the king of Rome, Prince of Parma, and duke of Reichstadt, the son of Napoleon I and Marie Louise never ruled France, though his father abdicated in his favor.

NAPOLEON III (Charles Louis Napoleon Bonaparte), 1808-1873: Emperor of the French, 1852-1870, son of Louis Bonaparte, King of Holland, nephew of Napoleon I.

PARMA, DUCHESSE DE (Louise Marie Thérèse d'Artois), 1819-1864: Daughter of the Duc de Berry, assassinated in 1820, and of Marie Caroline des Deux Siciles, sister of the Comte de Chambord. She was exiled after the 1830 revolution. In 1845 she married the hereditary Prince of Lucques who became Duc de Parma in 1849. The Duc de Parma was assassinated in 1854 and she became regent for her son Robert. When the duchy of Parma was annexed the Duchesse de Parma took refuge with her brother in Austria where she died five years later.

PIRON, ALEXIS, 1689-1773: Poet who wrote the play *Arlequin-Deucalion* (1722). He was elected in 1753 to the French Academy but Louis XV refused to ratify his election.

PITT, WILLIAM, 1759-1806: English statesman. Was Prime Minister for almost 20 years under George III.

PIUS IX, 1792-1878: Italian-born Giovanni Maria Mastai-Ferretti was elected to the papacy in 1846, at which time he took the name Pius IX. His was the longest pontificate of history, 1846-1878.

POUSSIN, NICOLAS, 1594-1665: This French painter went to Italy in 1624 and gained renown during the 16 years he remained in that country. At the request of Louis XVIII he returned to Paris where he worked for both Louis and Richelieu at the Louvre. He went back to Rome in 1643 and there spent the rest of his life. Primarily a classical painter, Poussin's best-known works include "Woman Taken in Adultery," "The Holy Family," "The Vision of Saint Paul," and "The Deluge."

RACINE, JEAN BAPTISTE, 1639-1699: French dramatist who produced a number of great works including *Les Plaideurs, Britannicus, Bérénice, Phèdre, Esther,* and *Athalie,* all of which are still produced today.

REGNARD, JEAN FRANÇOIS, 1655-1709: On one of his many travels through Europe, this French author was captured by Barbary pirates and held in slavery a year until the desired ransom was received. Known as a comic dramatist, his works include *Les Folies amoureuses, Le Légataire universel,* and *Les Ménéchmes.*

ROUSSEAU, JEAN JACQUES, 1712-1778: French writer, musician, and philosopher. His great work on political science, *The Social Contract,* appeared in 1762, together with *Emile,* his work on education. Because of his revolutionary views he was forced to leave Paris first to Switzerland and then to England. He settled in Wootton, Staffordshire, and wrote his *Confessions.* He returned to France in 1770.

SCHILLER, JOHANN CHRISTOPH FRIEDRICH VON, 1759-1805: German poet, dramatist, and historian. Schiller studied law and medicine and became a regimental surgeon in 1780. He also wrote poetry during that time and a play *Die Rauber* which was presented at Mannheim. Goethe and Schiller, who were close friends, are considered the most important figures in German literature of the time.

SÉVIGNÉ, MARQUISE DE (Marie de Rabutin-Chantal), 1626-1696: This woman of letters has given us much insight into the France of her time. Her correspondence, published in full in 1868, is composed of over 1,500 letters, most of them addressed to her daughter, the Comtesse de Grignan, who lived in the south of France. These letters are full of literary, social, and personal news and show the humor of their author as well as her elegant style.

STAËL, MME. DE, 1766-1817: The full name of this French-Swiss author was Anne Louise Germaine Necker, Baronne de Staël-Holstein. Her husband was the Swedish diplomat, Baron de Staël-Holstein. Her autobiography, *Dix Années d'exil,* was published in 1821.

TALMA, FRANÇOIS JOSEPH, 1763-1826: French actor. Greatest tragedian of his time, he made important reforms in costuming and technique and was admired by Napoleon and Louis XVIII.

TARENTE, DUC DE (Jacques Étienne Joseph Alexandre Macdonald), 1765-1840: He came from a Scottish family to become Marshal of France.

TAYLOR, ZACHARY, 1784-1850: Twelfth President of the United States, born in Orange County, Virginia. Taylor was elected President in 1848 on the Whig ticket. He died sixteen months later.

VICTORIA (Alexandrina Victoria), 1819-1901: Queen of England.

VOLTAIRE, assumed name of FRANÇOIS MARIE AROUET, 1694-1778: French author and philosopher, Voltaire was known as a brilliant wit.

WASHINGTON, GEORGE, 1732-1799: First President of the United States.

WELLINGTON, 1ST DUKE OF (Arthur Wellesley), 1769-1852: English soldier and statesman, Wellington joined the army in the year 1787 and by 1800 had become a major general. With the aid of Blücher he defeated Napoleon at Waterloo.

WILLIAM II (Willem Frederik George Lodewijk) 1792-1840: The son of William I, William II reigned as King of the Netherlands and Grand Duke of Luxembourg. During the Peninsular War he served with Wellington, and he was wounded at Waterloo. In the Belgian revolution of 1830 he was the leader of the Dutch Army.

WILLIAM II, 1626-1650, Prince of Orange. In 1641 he married Mary, eldest daughter of Charles I of England. William II died from smallpox and was succeeded by his posthumous son, William III of England.

YORK, 3RD DUKE OF (Richard Plantagenet), 1411-1460: This English statesman was appointed regent of France in 1436 under Henry VI. Two of his sons became kings of England: Edward IV and Richard III.

BIOGRAPHY OF MODERN
MEDALLISTS AND SCULPTORS

COËFFIN or HERBERT-COËFFIN, JOSETTE. Born in Rouen, France, December, 16, 1907. Studied at the Ecole des Beaux-arts in Rouen. Worked for the Manufacture de Sèvres (1937-1948). Her works can be seen at the Rouen Museum, the Villa Médicis at Sèvres, the Museum of Modern Art in Paris, in South America, the United States and Japan. Among her creations we find: the Golden Virgin at Gisors, France, the St. Joseph Virgin at Montreal, Canada, the bust of Tristan Bernard at the Paris Comédie Française, Medals of René Coty, President of the French Republic, of Joan of Arc, Jean Cocteau, General Ingold, General de Gaulle, President of the French Republic.

Mrs. Coëffin is Officer of the Legion of Honor, Chevalier of the Arts and Letters, Chevalier of the Mérite Civil. She is a prize-winner of the Guggenheim Foundation of New York, and was awarded a gold medal at the International Exhibition of 1937.

DAVID, ALBERT, born in 1896 at Liernais, Cote d'Or, France. Attended the Paris Ecole des Beaux Arts. First Prize of the City of Paris and of the Seine Department Medal at the International Competition for the Olympic Games; Gold Medal at the Salon des Artistes Français. Sculptor for several monuments dedicated to the Dead of World War I and to the members of the French Resistance in World War II. A number of medals for the French Mint and for Baccarat. Officer of the Legion of Honor in 1947.

HOLMGREM, LEO, born in Paris, France, in 1904. Studied at the Stockholm Art Academy where he received, in 1930, the Academy's highest award, a gold medal. Leo Holmgrem studied under Carl Milles and Lucien Bazon at the French Mint in Paris. In 1944 he joined the Royal Mint in Stockholm, Sweden, where he produced several medals and coins and also modern sculptures.

MAAR, DORA. Member of a surrealist circle in 1934, and a photographer of great talent. After she met Picasso in 1935, she worked closely with him for many years as a painter and sculptor.

POILLERAT, GIBERT, born at Mer, Loir-et-Cher, France, in 1902. He studied decorative arts in Paris at the Collège Technique Boulle, majoring in sculpture-engraving. After making jewelry in a Paris atelier he turned to the creation of wrought-iron objects and became one of the principal collaborators of the master ironworker, Edgar Brandt. In 1945 the French Government called upon him to design and produce the Collier de l'Ordre de la Libération. Poillerat was appointed to a Professorship at the Ecole Nationale Supérieure des Arts Décoratifs in 1947. He is Chevalier de la Legion d'Honneur.

SIMON, GEORGES, born in Paris, France, in 1906. He studied under the direction of the sculptor Grégoire as early as 1919 and won in 1927 the Paris Award. In 1951 he became engraver at the French Mint and won several medals from 1935 to 1951 including a gold medal in 1946 at the Salon des Artistes Français. Among his best-known works we find the medals of Robespierre, Schubert, Albert Schweitzer, City of Narbonne, University of Nice, Michelangelo.

BIBLIOGRAPHY

Bergstrom, Evangeline H. *Old Glass Paperweights* (New York, 1949).

Emperauger, J. P. *Verres et Cristaux Incrustés* (Paris, 1909).

Forrer, L. *Biographical Dictionary of Medallists* (England, 1904-16).

Greppe, Pascal. *Propos d'un collectionneur Napoléonisant* (Claye-Souilly, France, 1929).

Herbert, W. L. and Way. Articles in *The Connoisseur* (February 1922, September 1923, February 1924, January 1925, and June 1925).

Johannet, Edmond. Article on Andrieu in *L'Art* (Paris, 1883).

Jokelson, Paul. *Antique French Paperweights* (New York 1955).

———. *One Hundred of the Most Important Paperweights* (New York, 1967).

Nixon, J. "Glass Incrustation Cameos." Article in *Antique Collector* (London, 1932).

Paperweight Collectors' Association Bulletins (1954-67).

Pazaurek, Gustav E. Glaser. *Der Empire—Und Biedermeierzeit* (Leipzig, 1923).

Pellatt, Apsley. *Curiosities of Glass-Making* (London, 1849).

———. *Glass Manufactures* (London, 1821).

Revi, Albert Christian. *Nineteenth Century Glass* (New York, 1959).

INDEX